Accepting Goodbye
Living the Full Life

Jack Dawson, MD

Copyright © 2015 Jack Dawson, MD
All rights reserved.

ISBN: 0983857326
ISBN 13: 9780983857327
Library of Congress Control Number: 2014922597
NightLight Publishing Incorporated, Atlanta, GA

Contents

To the Reader		v
1	Death	1
2	Contemplating Death	6
3	Preparing for Death Enriches Life	11
4	Saying Goodbye: Make It Personal—Do It Now	21
5	Death and Dying: The End Is Near	30
6	Hospice and Palliative Care: The Details of Dying	44
7	Grieving and Mourning	57
8	Managing Life's Journey: Health and Aging	72
9	Disease	88
10	Continuing in the Struggle	103
Appendix A		113
References		117
Recommended Reading		119
Acknowledgments		121
About the Author		123

To the Reader

Our sights are on dying and death, but the target is living the full life.

Accepting death and responding to it has changed over time. Probably a significant change is that dying now occurs in hospitals rather than at home. The act of dying has not changed, but the milieu has and is evolving; thus, we evolve with it. It seems that everything changes over time. Even we change. The effects of technological advances, the growth of media, and the speed of information around the world have changed and have outpaced our models for communication. It seems that conflicts at home and in the world are increasing, and hard times for many persist.

An individual's ability to keep up and function normally is strained. Living a full, successful, healthy, and happy life is always a goal. But every project, every event, every goal, and every special night out comes to an end. Every life has its ending. Though death is not a production line, it can seem that way as we age and it happens so quickly to our loved ones and others. Our own turn will come.

Accepting Goodbye guides you, the reader, with facts, stories, questions, and commentary and is offered to enrich your life. The book may not answer all your questions, but it will assist you in your thinking and planning for dying and death so you can make wise choices going forward. And whatever life you have left, whether you are young or old, may you live it to the fullest.

While death frees one from pain and suffering, living life to the fullest with the opportunity to build more memories and experiences also brings freedom from many burdens. Of course, a decent quality of life to the end is gained by planning and preparing for the best of health as one ages. A full life brings understanding of who you are, knowledge of boundaries and tenets for living, freedom from unchecked reactionary and defensive emotions, such as angst and anger, and allows one to accept and love, which is the essence of life. Without harboring negative emotions and behaviors from what is termed our darker side, one is free to devote all of one's self for the purpose of being true, to give without obligation, and to be enabled to do the "right thing." The concept of a full life is expanded further in the book and you, the reader, may find freedom to develop it even further. Toward this effort immerse yourself to find your own definition and philosophy of living to the full. Savor the experience, for the resulting energy and wisdom created may enable you to live through the overflow. Though we shine a light on death, the emphasis remains on living. Death is best left in the background; it should not, however, become an unspoken, occult part of life.

1
DEATH

Whether you're dying, contemplating death, or facing the death of a loved one, thinking about what you want and understanding what is happening as events unfold will help you plan and will guide you during the experience. *Accepting Goodbye* is a guide to accepting the inevitability of death and gaining the courage to face it. It attempts to reconcile the reader to her or his own death and to the death of loved ones. In the case of your death, you can outline what you want, and in the event of your loved one's death, you can see that his or her wishes are carried out.

Death is the last barrier in life, a wall, yet it is a threshold to be crossed. Like any process, humans' interactions with dying have gradually changed over time (see Aries in References). To review, in antiquity, people accepted death as part of destiny without emotion or fanfare. One's final breath occurred in bed, at home. Long before last wills and testaments, dying people delegated their belongings where they desired, and no one contested the decisions. It was a time when they could make amends by forgiving others of wrongdoings. Initially, the person was not told the true nature of his condition and prognosis, but later, it was found best to be truthful and to not withhold information.

Many other details evolved, such as who was to be in attendance, confirmation the person was indeed dead, the position of the body—on the back looking upward with eyes closed and hands crossed upon the chest—and the burial after a short delay. There has always been a preference for separating the living from the dead; thus, cemeteries were positioned outside of town. (The thought at the time was that the added distance inhibited the dead from coming home to disturb the living and protected the townspeople from the malodorous decay.) It was popular for the grave site to be near a church, especially one containing a revered person such as a saint or other hero. The gruesome and frightening images surrounding death have been misinterpreted, for they serve as guards and protectors—scarecrows—to keep death away. Thus, the meanings of these images are the opposite of what they depict and reflect more a love of life and a dread of dying. With that in mind, death becomes less frightening.

Over the last millennia, attention was directed more toward the individual and what kind of life the person lived. Dying people of means—not the peasants—often visualized themselves as failures in life because they had not attained their youthful goals. They were thus unwilling to die and leave the accumulated comforts. Attention focused on the deceased's value to the family. Thus, in the burial preparations, attention was given to the person's standing in life, which was depicted in the design and cost of the casket, grave site, tomb, and the inscriptions thereon. Tombs and embellished inscriptions with pictures of the deceased have faded from view, and currently, there is less information at the grave site.

In reacting to death, an outward show of emotions was accepted in the early Middle Ages. Such reactions became muted until the eighteenth and nineteenth centuries, when changes occurred in family dynamics. Relationships evolved based on feelings and affection. Therefore, emotional reactions were equally as great when someone in another family died. People began reacting hysterically with expressed emotions, an exaggeration and a break in social conventions for the time. Currently, the behavior is mixed. Some react quietly, and others are less inhibited and publicly express emotions of mourning.

In the later 1900s, death shifted from home to hospital, where the patient was more isolated and alone. Death occurred there because the needed medical care could not be provided at home. Hospitals of the past were thought places to go to be "healed," and then they became the place where one was sent to die. Dying at home today might be preferred, but can we do that? It can be difficult and complicated to arrange, but it can be done.

Today, death and dying is a large, successful business. There are legal, medical, and funeral industry issues to consider. The last will and testament protects the dying and the family. It erases questions of mistrust that requests might not be respected.

The funeral arrangements are best decided long before the need, when all are more healthy and able to reason through the best choices. The funeral-home contract, embalming, casket, and headstones or footstones are items for purchase. Each is a choice. There's no law that governs the choices. The United States is one of the few countries in the world where embalming the dead is so popular—and why? Casket expenses seem to be excessive—why? Is it necessary that these traditions be continued as they are, or can they be readdressed and made less costly and more dependent on the wishes of all involved? This may explain the rise in cremation and distribution of ashes as a solution for burial. These expenses too can vary, depending on the choice of an independent company versus a funeral home.

Medical care is evolving too, with its focus on early diagnosis and treatment through combined efforts by engaged patients and medical providers. While today's patients appear sicker than in the past, perhaps because of delayed visits for care and increasing incidences of obesity, diabetes mellitus, and other diseases, in-hospital death rates from acquired infections are diminishing.

The problem may be the resistance of the dying one to lead the process. After all, this process is about her or him. They have opinions that need to be voiced. They can be addressed in lighter times, even years before their need. Perhaps then, the choices and pricing of the burial equipment can be more reasonable. One reason pricing might be driven upward is because the family's post-mortem choices are based on longstanding, occult feelings about family and the deceased.

While there are a number of events in life, including traumatic accidents or unnecessary illnesses, that contribute to death and influence one's memories, it's best not to focus on the worst. Memories are integrated with feelings that may lurk beneath the surface and influence decisions family members make for the deceased. In addition, past reactions of family members under stress predict future stress responses, and anger may be directed toward or against other family members as well. Practicing appropriate and anticipated behaviors for the patient and family to follow in advance of decline and sharing such expectations with the family can help, while focusing on desired memories can bring them to prominence. Time and continued efforts focusing on life encourage the worst images to fade and can influence remaining members to strive to live better lives.

The best time for individuals to focus on living is obviously while they are healthy. They can do this by making great memories, doing things for their own enjoyment, participating in habits necessary to maintain health, and living out their lives more meaningfully with family and friends close to them to the very end.

Should there be a penalty, such as a difference in insurance coverage or care, if his or her desires differ from recommendations based upon evidence-based guidelines? Changes are already evolving and more are expected, for at present, some insurance companies reward or penalize patients for results depending on smoking history and whether they are engaged in successful exercise and/or weight-loss programs. Compliance and positive results are important to keep costs down and to sustain wellness. The health costs for noncompliance may prove prematurely deadly, whereas focusing on understanding, compliance, and positive results will produce a well-earned reward of healthy living. Certainly, discussions with the experts, beginning with the doctor, are encouraged.

For us living, our turn will come, and our lives will end. We usually avoid conversations involving death because it is depressing and carries a morbid label. Meanwhile, if promoting death motivates us to get our houses in order, plan and prepare for it, begin living more meaningful lives, and nurture our relationships, then, if we begin this process soon enough, our efforts will promote living and prove worthwhile.

2
CONTEMPLATING DEATH

"DEATH IS NOT TO BE FOUGHT, BUT RATHER TO BE ACKNOWL-
EDGED AND USED TO ADVANTAGE, TO BE WORKED
WITH AND EVEN BE CONSULTED AS AN ALLY."
—*Martin Heidegger*

Death is part of living; often, one is able to observe signs that it's coming.

Many embrace death as they get older; when life's autumn turns to winter, they attend family and friend's funerals, or they become sicker and tire of the struggle.

They find comfort in the anticipated relief and approach it without fear, even though it is shrouded in unknowns.

When healthy and younger, how does one appreciate what a full life encompasses without contemplating, in contrast, the end: death?

Contemplating death allows one the opportunity to live the struggle differently.

As we age and desire retired life, we somehow perceive it as an extended, stress-free vacation, but with experience, we soon realize that struggles continue, making life hard to pursue with enjoyment.

We are in misery if attitudes aren't adjusted.

We are to face each challenge as life's journey has taught us; we deal with them utilizing all our skills as best we can.

The distinction between giving in and adjusting to change and giving up is determined by our purpose and efforts.

It is best to face both life and death without dread or depression, for without angst we are strengthened, which is valuable.

Our choices in life affect our attitudes, which in turn affect further decisions and planning. They affect our views and how we approach living and dying.

The decision to give up, if due, can bring sweet relief if we have suffered with prolonged pain and years of misery.

A better choice is to give in to the challenge—a problem with a relationship, a flare associated with disease or impending death—trading frustration and anger for calmness and clarity of thinking.

We may well die as we live; therefore, we should think things through and make the best choices while we live.

It is best to do our homework and plan.

Considering death

I have witnessed the deaths of persons I was close to and those I did not know.

The experiences have not made me less affected—I still grieve.
How can we accept dying as part of living?
Are we prepared?
When will the acceptance come?
We all die.
How can we prepare?

Has there been anything we have wanted to change but have not?
Why do we tend to maintain the status quo?
Have we begun to change?
Do we need to?
How does one do that?

Was death ever viewed as an anticipated stage in life?

And when we do not help ourselves or change, are we preferring misery and death?

Goodbyes

Goodbyes in love and death are both hard.

Both end in heartbreak.

Once bonds are broken in love, meaningful visions, beliefs, and faith can crumble.

Once bonds are broken in death, meaningful visions, beliefs, and memories can magnify.

Hard losses necessitate rebuilding.

The essence of human life is in the individual's spirit, even in death.

Memories harbor the power of love.

Relationships

Life is about relationships that transcend the individuals.

Relationships make memories, allow us to give and receive love, and make it possible for us to live in the hearts and minds of others when alive and also after we die; our influence and spirit live on.

Specifically, our mind's eye has the ability to re-create people in our memories, whether alive or dead. If they're not with us and we need them, we summon them to us through our imaginations.

What does this need mean—what does it say about us?

We progress through many changes in relationships, especially with a spouse.

Preparing to say goodbye meaningfully can take a lifetime, even with a long-standing, intimate relationship.

You can know someone so well, it's as though your genetics have intermingled.

You eventually may develop similar gestures in your words and actions.

"Soul mate" enmeshment is healthy if each person stays independently dependent.

It behooves couples to have a meaningful and deep conversation about life, including details about death and saying goodbye.

Did we realize we would miss them so?

Preparing

What do we do before they die?
    What do we do after their deaths come?
    What do we do before we die?
    If we die first, will they miss us?
    Did they know and feel our love?
    What are we to be remembered for?
    What do we want to be remembered for?
    Were we there for others?
    Did they know they meant that much to us?
    Did we reveal the depth of our love?
    Did we live the full life?
    Were we good examples for them?
    Did the changes we made, if any, influence them?

Quality of life and death are interconnected

Death will occur whether we lead the good and full life or not, whether we live as a saint or not. Death is guaranteed.

What we desire is both quality and quantity in life.

There are some things about death that can be the way we want them to be, but we have to speak up. We have to plan.

For that's where we're to focus.

If I am determined, will my vision of the rest of my life and the quality of my death have an effect on how I live my life now?

Can I affect the quality and duration of both my death and my life each and every day by what I do today?

Does what we individuals do really matter?

Are you asking yourself that question?
If not, it is time you did.

Milestone events and a softened heart

After life-threatening illnesses, many patients report experiencing a subjective peace of mind in spite of knowing they will inevitably die.

They find that life's hard struggles and challenges continue, and they will progressively need more assistance to live.

They loosen their grip even more on the controls that the events, diseases, and age take from them.

They desire to return to their old selves but know they cannot, for there is no going back.

As life wanes, the person mourns—self-grief in action.

They learn to carry the damaged selves with them and often ask, "How much more can I take; how much longer?"

They continue in their struggles.

We experience a recurring cycle in life of loss followed by renewal; we are knocked down and always strive to stand and keep going; the will to live is a strong drive.

As though we are phoenixes, we first seek life; we then focus more on dying, anticipating it as a welcome relief.

In life, we live, we die.

The essence of life—relationships

Life's experiences increase our sense of awareness for relationships; they give life its essence and purpose until death.

Therefore, we are driven to survive and improve life—day by day.

In your pursuits, refresh your thinking—combine dying and death with living; make the whole process of dying as important to us as are life and relationships, for one is a reflection of the other.

When we combine dying and death with living, they become part of family life and the larger family experience: community.

3
Preparing for Death Enriches Life

The loved one is the subject of one's affection, the one who is dying or who has died, but the loved ones are also the heirs of the one we are focusing upon.

Many ways to die

Examples:

(1) "I've called you in because I've decided to die and want to know you'll be OK without me. Yes, I've held on for a while, but I'm just too tired to go on. Life in this nursing home isn't worth living." After they gave her their consent, their mom stopped taking her medications, stopped eating and drinking, and, in three days, she died.

(2) He felt so sleepy yet was sick on his stomach. But spurred on in his rage, he still vowed to get even. The overdose was working, and no one was to know that he needed help.

(3) "Call hospice. I'm not going through chemo. I'd rather die."

(4) "But I want to live; I have so many things to live for and so many things I need to do. Please help me." There were no further treatment options. She was dying.

Determined death, drug overdose, avoiding suffering, fear of dying; each example and the cases listed elsewhere—everyone has his or her own story.

Death anywhere and everywhere brings sadness, disaster, and tragedy—too much to bear. Terrible misfortunes for the victims. Overwhelming losses for the survivors.

There are many ways to die. And, as in living, some have a choice, and others do not. Death is inevitable. For many, it is a portal to a new frontier, and for others, a destination. For many, death merges our beliefs and hopes for a spiritual life after death.

All known civilizations have shown evidence that the people dealt with separation from life. This is part of being human. The tradition has lasted for eons with differing details depending on the culture.

Our hope is to combine living with dying, as both are huge parts of life. Separating them is similar to the separation of mind and body. They are kept apart when they are part of the same: life. With the struggles we face, love and death are givens in life, but we often do not make the most of them. It is possible we do not understand what living the full life means.

Death may cause family conflicts to resurface

It is sad that brokenness has more prominence in our lives. Our hurts and fears well up in response to family strife, sickness, and death. Often, somewhere between the onset of acute illness of our loved one and the distribution of assets, longstanding, hidden jealousies and grudges resurface in families. These reactions were, of course, laid down long before; we are reminded of this time and time again. The seething, grieving ones certainly were not parented by or taught by their culture to appreciate life by living it day to day as if it were their last, or by living out an ethic of serving others.

Allowing issues associated with death more emphasis in life, might we attend more to living and the important relationships in the family? There will be many opportunities to revisit, influence, and nurture, if only we will spend time with specific individuals in need. By experiencing the gift of love, they may find the undercurrents of brokenness are soothed, and their behavior in the moment will be appropriate. I, for one, choose to focus on love and remain active to nurture all family relations. This work is an attempt to meld all the parts into one life, to be a resource to assist both the one dying and the survivor(s) through the maze of events, to review many of the details needed so life for the living does not seem to stop, and to allow one to continue the struggle through the fog of grief to face life's challenges. If previously discussed, it would be helpful for the survivors to remember what the deceased wanted them to do at this time and in their absence.

Couples

Couples have a special relationship. It consists of two different people uniting with the potential to help each other complete their maturation and become one. They are able to maturate because they live life in the service of their relationship. They marry until "death do us part."

Renewed life for survivors

These life-ending events are sad and life altering but are nonetheless part of life's cycle. In that concept, these persons might best be viewed as having an opportunity to live on as a survivor. Remembering the discussions in preparation for the challenges ahead brightens a darker period of life. Though grief will still be a challenge, through preparedness, at least some of this process—taking care of individuals—mirrors the lifestyle the couple lived and the character they developed through their bond and enlightens the memories they shared. This is possible because the individuals were and still are part of each other. Life and death bring opportunities for growth and present challenges for both the individual and the couple, whether it is happening to them or to those significant individuals around them. These are components of an evolving process toward the full life as we individuals, couples, families, and generations come and go.

We, indeed, have a tall responsibility and duty to guide those coming behind us. Death is not to be dreaded any more than winter. Death, as the final season of life, is to be embraced and prepared for, similar to the way we prepare for winter. Being prepared includes assisting our families to understand what we want and how to go about doing it. It assures them that we love them, forgive them, and thank them for what they have done and that we anticipate that they will remember our requests for them after we die. We urge change: the death experience will be different for all, to be viewed differently. Discussing death when healthy is an opportunity for change, enlightenment, and growth. It needs to be practiced in a new and different way through more openness and with a specific focus on fostering healthier relationships.

In group, most victims of heart attacks and life-threatening heart procedures have discovered renewal. For them, life changes for the better. The individuals are now healthier in spite of their experiences. Each individual has taken his or her old self, blended it with the damaged self, and created an overall improved, mellower, and softened self, a new balance. Their near-death experiences have uncovered a new appreciation for life. They clearly realize they will die one day, and, until then, they will live it fully.

The opportunity to enrich life is certainly present the moment death gets any attention. After all, for what other reason would one prepare a bucket list? The list may contain things to do, but to be complete, it would also include relational goals as well. While on the quest to complete one's list or after having fulfilled the list, one has a new outlook. The individual is determined and anticipates being able to carry on living the life he or she wants to live.

Legacy

And what about our goals for legacy? Are we willing to work as hard for legacy as we are to work on the bucket list? How great will we feel after that accomplishment, knowing it will take years to plan and implement? Certainly, each of us desires to leave behind something of value that is not included in the material things we will leave. If we desire to influence others, especially their hearts, we need time and patience to think it through, a vision of what it will look like, an idea of the future success of the influence, and the work to make it happen, for legacy does not occur haphazardly. So what is our legacy? Have we prepared anything specific? Do we understand the ways we have influence?

Legacy is influence

If we could live out our inherent kindness in life, we might better show the love within us through our words, attitudes, and actions. Thus, our own spirit would not only influence others to live as we live, but it will continue after our death. Even the subtle changes we make in life may influence others. The more we change for the better—calming down, becoming softer of heart and gentler—the more positive influence we give. Our individual change has influence, for any change conceivably has broad effects that spread to others by varying degrees. Our influence in our death and as dust does not simply sit still; it acts like an engine that propels it to stir with a wind of its own. This drives the influence. So, through our changes in life, our dust blows with a gentle wind carrying our living spirit to others. Our winds of change do not settle on others with any fog of unsettling uncertainty, but they encourage through gentle breezes of our influence with a rhythm of our own fashion. Any visible changes made as we aged, when we finally had more understanding of life and relationships—the important things—provide an upgrade for attitudes, habits, behaviors, and traditions for our loved ones to grow from.

It is a benefit for us, as we live through the different stages of our lives, to keep in mind our influence on our loved ones, for they are right there in front of us and watching. They have thoughts and feelings, and you can bet they are recording and processing your, my, and everybody else's influence in their lives. They too make connections and are influenced by others who give them the time to connect with them. Being aware of them and continuing our own efforts to be present in the family and to keep changing for the better is difficult at best when pursuing a career and maintaining a family. However, it is part of being a leader, a partner, and a parent. We need to continuously monitor ourselves, and, however busy we are, we need to connect, for our children and spouses are the nuclei for our families' communities. As in any meaningful relationship, when the two parties connect, they have to be engaged at a certain level. A unique method to document whether or not the connection is made is to read the nonverbal signs and simply ask them how things are going between the two of you.

We want to influence people. We cannot force it on others. We can only offer it as a gift. They may take it readily if they trust us and believe we are there for them, or they may let it be and contemplate it. That we placed it out there with no tension attached is important. They will make use of the gift when they are ready. Since we realize that our influence is only a gift for them to use at their discretion, we will patiently leave it there with no strings attached and no expectations. When conversing, clarity and speech structure expresses our expectations.

Our influence is analogous to the difference in hearing and listening—our youth and those we leave behind are the ones who have to receive, absorb, and assimilate our influence. All growth is a process. Like gardening, it proceeds step by step. If you wait and observe closely, the influence that generates any change may not be detectable until later. Over time, one sees more obvious evidence of the living growth. Think of the thrill of changes resulting from your influence that occur later, even after you die. Your small influence extrapolates into significant change in them. All you want is to begin the process. Your overall influence may well produce more than you would have imagined or understood when you gave it. It is the true essence of living life to the fullest, and it brings the potential for living forever.

Legacy is honoring our dead

We honor those we leave behind. Our efforts to change, even a little, will not go in vain. Any good influence we have had on others honors us. Being honored and held up by families is the norm in many cultures. Asian families honor their ancestors by enshrining them in their homes. The parents and grandparents live on in memories. They foster continuity and family traditions. In life's latter years, the young adults expect to care for the older ones. Through these traditions, we experience the essence of family in community.

Legacy is a tradition of renewal

There is a need for continuous improvement—to be refreshed. We do this in our secular and in our religious lives. Take, for instance, the act of sponsoring memorial flowers at religious services, honoring the dead at memorial holidays, repeating marriage vows, attending class reunions—all done as acts of renewal. Some of these activities honor our pasts, and others help us move forward. These events are certainly not seen as dark and morbid but as vivid reminders recommitting us to the full spectrum of life. The ritual of the events connects us to the lives of both ordinary people and "heroes" from our past. It is an act that further shows community.

Renewal is possible when we include death and dying in our focus as a vital part of life. The individual acts are done in love. By continuing these honors for the dead and by continuing to live by our faith and beliefs, we can be better prepared to die. This emphasizes the importance of how we treat one another, for we die as we have lived. These are the traditions that expand our family and community—the essence of living.

Legacy is in traditions and influence

For those who believe in a higher power:

All religions address death and a life thereafter. To consider the Abrahamic religions, Jews focus more on life here and now, though there is clear evidence in the Torah of belief in existence after death, with separation of destinations for the righteous and the wicked.

For Muslims, life is a preparation for the eternal life to come. Allah gives humans free will, yet they carry the responsibility for their actions into their afterlife. The human soul dies by Allah's leave. On the Day of Judgment, Allah is to balance the good deeds a person has done in his or her life against the bad deeds. They view Allah as a kind god with hopes that most reside in paradise and only the worst of the wicked are condemned to Hell.

From the Christian perspective, Jesus was victorious over death at the Resurrection; thus, death has been overcome. In death, Christians' earthly bodies return to dust. While living, through faith, Christians receive the gift and allow it to change their lives. With death, they join Christ in heaven.

Though atheists do not believe in God or in an afterlife, they die. They live their lives in the here and now with no preconceived notions or expectations for life after death; with death, all existence is complete.

So death, for some, is a destination, and for others, a bridge.

Thus, in living and dying, dying is the only thing that is guaranteed, which is another reason to make it part of living and to make the most out of life while we can.

Legacy is the gift of love

Love is powerful when unleashed and is able to counter opposing negative forces. Love always protects, trusts, hopes, and perseveres.

Love is the polar opposite of nothingness, lifelessness, and indifference. Anger and hate oppose love but are at the same end of the pole. Emotional anger and conditional love change abruptly, depending on circumstances, like happy and sad, likes and dislikes, yes and no.

Love presents as four types: kinship, friendship, romance, and unconditional love—selfless or divine. We humans usually have excessive amounts for ourselves and become entrapped with our own importance. Love is accompanied by expressions of caring, kindness, attraction, and affection. Love can be intimate, and, even without the erotic chemistry, sweet. It is a pleasure to know, give, and receive love—a special interaction. When encountered, do you engage closeness with others or reject them by becoming withdrawn or anxious? Do your chemicals lead to calm or urge you not to eat, to be nervous, or to run? Love is part of us—our anatomy and function. Love in the moment changes those involved. It can tame and mold. It provides a focus and vision for others, namely our spouses, children, family, and those chosen meaningful relationships.

Love is life. Love is peace. Love conquers evil. Love is people—relationships. Love extends beyond life and into death.

Love, through meaningful relationships and supporting memories, extends the deceased's life, the loved one, within the minds and hearts of those left behind—the deceased's loved ones. Love connects loved ones and extends those connections far beyond the individuals. The sum is far greater and more powerful than the individual parts. The influence of love gained, especially unselfish and unconditional love, is infectious. It is natural to love and to express it. Our love is akin to our spirit, and spirit transcends all human capacities.

Love brings peace. It can render one's heart to softness and openness to push beyond the self and reach out to others. We are then enabled to reveal ourselves beyond our protective armor so others, especially our loved ones, will know us as we really are deep inside. Through the act of doing something for someone else, love overcomes. Love overcomes the urge to only take care of the self and opens each person's heart to reach beyond the self. This can break and replace vicious cycles with circles of love and kindness. As a result, we can grow beyond ourselves. Enabling these characteristics makes us both whole in life and whole as we transcend spiritually into death, and for many, into a new life.

4
Saying Goodbye: Make It Personal— Do It Now

Encompass goodbyes in life

Saying goodbye while our loved one is alive seems awkward and out of place, but it also seems the right thing to do and a pleasant task. It may be difficult, especially if we realize the end is upon us. It is best done, of course, while all are living. It is easier if talking is a regular routine, if there has been a form of closure: if regrets and sorrows have been fleshed out, if bad feelings of unfairness and arguments are discussed and left at a point of arbitration, if caregiving has been shared with a perception that the support system worked, that all possible was done for optimal care, and if the one cared for was able to share thanks and appreciation to those caring for her or him. That, indeed, is a tall order, but it is possible, and many families work through it successfully. It depends on the patterns of familial behaviors embedded within the family archives. As heartbreak and hurts linger, guilt and anger override any chance for peace, and more conflict occurs. Outcomes then follow reactive patterns learned over the years. These are outworn, recycled behaviors that will hurt both the person(s) reacted toward and the one(s) reacting.

It is always helpful to discuss these issues with all involved—in a family meeting—to clarify the likelihood of sickness developing, how far to go with the evaluation and treatments, and the possibilities of complications that might stall the recovery process. Dying and end-of-life issues are more than private matters. Though it's personal to the patient, the entire family will benefit by being included, especially if the dying one takes a leadership role. Going forward, each person can consider his or her own situation in a healthy way over time. This is, of course, when it's important to discuss the details of the living will and the medical, durable power of attorney selection. This will allow time for the family to discuss with the doctor the likelihood of a disaster occurring and get his or her thoughts and advice on the subject. Remember, it is not always the older members who succumb to these issues. It happens to the younger ones too. The process of life and death is not based on longevity or privilege, and though it is likely that the old and weak are more vulnerable, it is best to consider all possibilities and be prepared.

Couples share a harmonious balance

Couples balance each other. It can be an efficient rhythm, part of the "dance" forged through growth over time. The balance defines a complementary relationship: it's couple-choreographed. Some of us learn to lead and may switch back and forth, or one dominates and toes get bruised. Ideally, we adjust and simply dance. The balance is the essence of a couple's strength, encompassing each member's being, meaning they influence each other. The influence may include fostering improvement in health and lifestyle and eagerness to acquire experience and knowledge; calming emotions; and improving tolerance, patience, willingness, ability to cope and cooperate, and ability to listen and plan—to get along.

Are we standing independently? How much are we leaning on each other? Leaning as needed is OK, for we're independently dependent. But, after a death of one partner, how easily will the survivor cope and adapt to such a different life?

Through discussions, my wife and I both view that future, living alone, as one we will eventually be OK with. We are both strong in our own right, but which one of us is providing the primary strength and which one is sharing the energy? Often a family's strength rests with the woman. The balance, the dance, and the bonds are gifts that may be of no concern now, for we have shared satisfaction in our full life. Hidden signs could exist, however, that might predict a difficult time of adjustment for one of us. At present, we have the time to begin more preparations. The thing for us to do now is to keep talking and giving toward that preparedness.

My wife and I assume the survivor will grieve and recover. We have all our fond memories and the backing of our family and friends. How do we feel about our survivor moving on and going forward, seeking an independent life? What does that mean? Does that include a newfound relationship in the future?

I can only love her now, demonstrate it, and continue to share with her in our full life. I have assured her that I have bared my life and soul and would want her to continue having the opportunity to be free. We have our special moments, experiences, and memories. If held to those, she would lose ground and be living in our past, bound. With death, our marriage vows are broken. With my death, she will be free, and that freedom defines the opportunity to open herself to new relationships and what they may bring to her.

I have experienced women and men who have "given their all" to their spouses during many years of illness. The problem is that they sacrifice themselves and lose their own identity through giving their services, especially if an illness is prolonged or with hardships, or if the spouse is mistreated. This often makes it difficult to recover and recharge after the death. If I am the one who dies first and time permits, we are to do everything possible to take care of me and simultaneously maintain my spouse's independence by encouraging her to have her own schedule and life, which is the way we have lived. If circumstances interfere and I need more assistance, then I have to be as cooperatively independent as I can be and be ever thankful for her care when given.

Whether she or I is the stronger one, we want her to experience fulfillment from the fruits of all her labors that have undergirded and supported our relationship all these years. We have worked toward those goals. We are sure it will require continued efforts to sustain them during our waning times until death do us part.

Before death

Parting and saying "I love you"

What is the reason we say, "I love you," and kiss goodbye so often when we leave each other? Is it a tradition—a simple, superficial gesture in case we die unexpectedly? Is it necessary every time we separate? What is the root meaning when we express it? Isn't it better to show we care, to live it rather than say it? But are there those we truly cherish, to whom we say it because we mean it? Certainly, there are times to discuss it face to face, but how often do we discuss such an important and meaningful subject? How often do we really mean it? I, for one, prefer to show my love and to make it count.

Parting on a good, positive note, as though you will never see each other again, without any lingering strife between you, and saying goodnight with a clear conscience, impacts your partner. It is as if you, not your partner, may be the one who will not return or wake in the morning. The thought and the action give more palpable meaning. It is the thing to do.

Celebrating life

Celebrations are possible when one is alive and well. Certainly, meaningful contact with family and friends through casual, festive gatherings is easily arranged. Then, the one having the party can focus on individual time with each invitee to share the true meaning of their relationship.

Write your own obituary

It is often a useful exercise to write your own obituary or for your spouse to write it as he or she discusses it with you. This task can be enjoyable, and it can begin the process of goodbyes. You can write the template long before the need arises. This gives you the opportunity to discuss your history and give details about your family, accomplishments, interesting experiences, education, and career. You write the important items that have occurred in your life and what training, traits, and talents have highlighted you as a person. The document is about who you are—your story, a way to remember you. This is your opportunity to reveal yourself for all to see and to steer the direction. It is far better to be personally involved rather than for someone else to observe superficially that you were "a good mechanic" and no more. This is meaningful information. It is worth the research and thought before the need. And it should be a fun experience.

After death

Though it is a party, it is cavalier to call it that. Celebration is preferred.

Obituary

If not written previously, the obituary is a summary, a story of the deceased's life. It is a narrative of his or her education, training, and accomplishments. It is told in a way that describes the uniqueness of the person, his or her character, why and how she or he is to be remembered, who the surviving family is, the reason for the death, and details about the funeral service and burial.

Funerals

Funerals comprise the announcement or obituary, the wake or visitation, the service, and the burial of the departed. It is a ceremony to remember and to honor the person who has died. They vary somewhat in various cultures around the world, but the basic tenets are similar. Some encourage a luncheon, and some request no flowers be sent, for it would sadly remind the family of the departed.

Many have told me that funerals are for the living and they attend funerals for themselves—to feel better, to clear their chests, particularly if they harbor any guilt. They say the dead are dead, their souls need praying for, and the families need to put their dead at rest with the aid, support, and respect of friends. Many attend for renewal, for the funeral mass is a Christian sacrament. Viewings and funerals give closure.

Memorials

Memorials are held when the body is absent—lost or cremated. It is a time to remember the dead at a later date.

A form of worship

We become upset, feel and show emotions of all kinds, or we sit quietly.
Underneath is the fact that the service is a meaningful form of worship, a sacrament, and not intended to center around our emotions or how best to make an experience out of it. It is not a performance. Through such worship, we show respect, love, and admiration for the person being honored and support his or her family.

Goodbyes

We may have our individual and preferred ways of saying goodbye. It is not something we get to practice. It may come sooner or later. It is impossible to explain how to plan it. In the days of yore, the burning pyre floated away for all to see. Yet we are different today and need closer bonds that represent the special and meaningful relationship.

It can be done in the processing of the funeral and burial, for it's a meaningful service, or by taking the trip your spouse promised you but because of acute illness or injury never got to complete. It could be represented by taking portions of the family on adventurous trips or other celebratory festivities. After the funeral, that home keeps getting bigger and bigger, maybe only serving to push one along.

Saying goodbye before death gives more fulfilling closure. But, as has been said before, we die as we live. And, to that point, what have our goodbyes been like on a day-to-day basis and when parting for real trips? Tradition is established and habits formed; the ruts are already in the road. Were you OK with the way it was then? Are you OK with it now? What will it be?

On the one hand, if you overrepresent it, will you feel better? If not, then ratchet it down. If you "blow it off" and do not do as much as you did before, will you feel more regret or more guilt?

Think about it and follow your heart. Do some of both, or continue doing the same. If you did say goodbye before your loved one died, it may keep coming back to you in the form of questions and doubts about whether you could have done more. Those thoughts are coming from your own negative self-talk and are best let go. Your loved one is not here and will rest in peace. The deceased may, as he or she might have done in life, appreciate your frugality, which will justify minimal expense, and that is "good." This is your goodbye and yours alone. You have all your memories, and that may be enough, for you simply need to get some distance and time between you and the final days, weeks, and months to bring the deceased back into view. A trip may be nice for lots of reasons. You may be able to enjoy your trip with others or enjoy one you anticipate in the near future; just realize your loved one's picture will not be a part of it. She or he is an integral part of your memories. As you return to a favorite and special place the two of you visited and raved about, that trip may surprise you and awaken you and your memories all the more. You will be OK!

Treasures

In the event that both spouses die, what does one do with all their belongings? If they did their homework, they have cleaned out their garage, basement, and attic; however, if not, there is even more junk or prized possessions to sort through. There will be large and small items to be distributed. Some are of sentimental significance only, items that have significance to one child or person much more than to another. Some families have successfully managed this issue by choosing the most vocal or emotionally affected members to be the major persons to list and separate all items in equal "piles"; they will be the last to choose their piles. This has had the best outcome.

Preparing for goodbye by utilizing the things that count

Ira Byock, MD, is an experienced physician who's written extensively about palliative and hospice care. In *The Four Things That Matter Most: A Book about Living*, he begins with a quote from John Greenleaf Whittier: "For of all sad words of tongue or pen, the saddest are these: 'It might have been!'"

With this phrase, Whittier acknowledges regrets observed in dysfunctional relationships. In dealing with the dying and their families, Dr. Byock emphasizes repair of disconnected or broken relationships by saying these phrases: "Please forgive me," "I forgive you," "Thank you," and "I love you." He says, "These four simple statements are powerful tools for improving relationships and life."

To quote from the Introduction of his book:

"The practice of goodbye—

> It's been said that life is a sexually transmitted condition with a terminal prognosis. Having worked for years in close proximity to death, I have come to understand viscerally that we live every moment on the brink. We are, each one of us, at every moment, a heartbeat away from death. Seen against the backdrop of our certain mortality, our differences are dwarfed by our commonality—and the importance we hold for one another."

5
Death and Dying: The End Is Near

"The question is not whether we will die, but how we will live."
—*Joan Bonysenko*

"Live as if you were to die tomorrow. Learn as if you were to live forever."
—*Mahatma Gandhi*

"Death is not the greatest loss in life. The greatest loss is what dies inside us while we live."
—*Norman Cousins*

"For me not to fight does not mean to give up. On the contrary, I embrace my life with more appreciation and affection than ever before. But fighting death as a full-time preoccupation squeezes out opportunities to embrace life as it is, as it comes, as a miraculous gift."
—*Forrest Church*

Dying is an expected part of life

Peers from other countries and cultures who work in the hospital setting have noticed the struggles we go through as we, individuals and families, approach and experience death. In their diverse countries, death is more a part of life than it is here. Their impression is that we deny death and let it catch us by surprise, that it resembles something forbidden, that we fear it. To them, generations come and go. "As with birth, in death we each have our turn. It's anticipated, we are fussed over, and then we're let go." The elders are revered and enshrined within the family. Survivors give up the body and the person but cherish the memories.

When we are critically ill and appear to be dying, so many things are happening. The whole experience is overwhelming even to the observer. When in the hospital, the sick patient suffers from weakness and exhaustion, and she or he cannot move freely because of the IV and monitoring leads and other tubes. Consciousness comes and goes. Some patients were in the grips of a serious infection with signs of toxicity; in shock after a severe cardiac event, with pneumonia and a racing heart rate; in a panic struggling to breathe in the intensive-care setting; suffering after a severe burn or after a motor-vehicle accident with multiple fractured ribs from chest trauma; and there are those who are miserably sick at home before accepting the need to go to the emergency room. Often, many of these patients recover.

Even after the patient is transferred out of the intensive care unit and on the floor preparing in their minds to go to rehab or home soon, the unexpected happens. The patient's heart goes into a deadly rhythm with essentially no effective blood flow, the blood pressure plummets, and the patient loses consciousness and dies. The emergency team jumps in to resuscitate, and if they are unsuccessful after a while utilizing strict protocol, the team stops its efforts and withdraws.

Another scenario is an unsuccessful response to all efforts to restore the patient from failing organs or from a severe stroke. The person had previously decided with his or her family to have no further aggressive treatments. The body does not respond, and the person deteriorates and quits breathing.

The moment of death

The doctor looks and listens for the absence of breathing, listens for the absence of the heart beating in the chest, and feels for the absence of neck pulses. If these findings are confirmed, she or he notes the time of day and, at that moment, pronounces the person dead.

Most religions view death as the moment the person's state as a human ends. The person is pronounced dead when there is absence of heartbeat, breathing, and brain function. When Abrahamic religion believers die, the spirits transcend to a more exalted and secure existence. Such a place is located in a heavenly paradise, protected from the grind and struggles of daily, worldly existence. Thus, human life transforms into spiritual life because of the belief that the change is of God. The alternative to such beliefs is our failure to exist except in memories.

Preparations

When given bad news in the form of a diagnosis and treatment options, you, as the patient, must ask for predictions and personal expectations. Though death can come quickly, for many given an unfavorable prognosis, life lingers. Whether you are told you have two weeks to live or that you will live a full life if you comply with the treatment recommendations, you must be informed as part of your ownership. You must know what to expect, for your stability, recovery, and risks of dying are based on the diagnosis and treatment options. You must be part of the decision-making process by asking about your status and expectations. What are the predicted timelines? What is the treatment plan in and out of the hospital, and what testing and treatment plans are recommended, if any? In the case of treatment, what type of treatment and how harsh will it be, and is a discussion about recovery time appropriate?

Begin the discussion with whomever you want to be in attendance with you, or, depending on circumstances, whomever you want to be kept in the communication loop. You want to be clear about your wishes.

Death is part of life

Our knowledge of death exists on this side of the wall, for we are alive. Thus, to us, death is part of life.

Life and death go hand in hand. Death not only brings the end, but for many, the hope of a new beginning. It comes too soon for some and too late for others. It brings relief, even escape. It brings sorrow, emptiness, and loss for those left behind.

Life and death are about grit—courage and perseverance, which are attributes needed to explore, to do the mundane, and to excel. Does our vigor in pursuing life while older match that when we were younger, before our wane? For most of our lives, we pursued life with abandon in regard to future consequences. Are we effective stewards of our futures? Do our futures include death? For it not only happens to others—the older folks, that is—but is often forgotten until "my turn comes."

Our aging process brings change. It is often wear and tear in organ systems in the presence of risk factors that create diseases. We are people with diseases, whatever our age. We, however, are not our diseases. The self is already defined; the disease does not change that. The disease may bring testing, medications, and follow-up. It may even bring pain, suffering, hospitalization, procedures, and special treatments. We may choose to have the full course of treatment or no treatment at all.

How long do I have?

Prognosticating, as a physician's skill, is developed over years of experience with patients and a variety of diseases followed to death's end. Dying is a slow process, or it can come more quickly, depending on many variables including specifics of disease survival; combinations of diseases pulling at the threads of life; and the individual's will to live, which is affected by years of circumstances meaningful to the patient's health and well-being. Certainly, evidence-based data may be helpful, but overall, people die. Some bear out predictions, and some do not. What's important is that patients, their families, and special friends take advantage of whatever time they are given for sharing, mending, and individual goodbyes.

We're all in the process of growth and decline, living and dying. The clock of life keeps ticking until the end. As if we are watching the seconds on a CD tick down until the song ends, so it may be at the end of our lives.

It does not appear we're accepting it well.

Read the obituaries. Why do we refer to dying as a "passing"? Is the soft-pedaling due to kindness or hesitancy to fully acknowledge our loved one's death? Were we involved in writing it?

We are familiar with graphs depicting human growth and decline—aging and the possibility of various bodily systems degenerating and deteriorating. Certain systems are more critical, and as they deteriorate, they may pull other systems under too, hastening the demise. We should recognize the signs and see change coming. Taking care of oneself extends into the older years—through our whole lifetimes. We are never too old to learn, to change, and to stay as active as we can. Retirement, whether forced or anticipated as the reward at the end of the rainbow, is time for good things—new and different activities, relaxation, and fun. Many take part with fulfillment, while life does not give others the privilege.

Hope

Hope has a place in death and life; it always fits in. Hope motivates, instills courage, and provides the thrust to accept, endure, and finish the task. There are many scenarios in which individuals did not die as predicted. It was only a prediction, an educated guess. They still chose to live, and hope was involved. Past a certain point, hope will not help prolong life but will assist the person to let it go. It may also enlighten one to have an enduring presence for those left behind as they die.

"Good" death

Death is an integral part of living and deserves consideration sooner than at life's end. There is a need to discuss the possible hereafter from the perspective of the loved one's religious beliefs and vision for what lies ahead. Discussions about events after death, such as wills and funerals, are to be held while your loved one is living.

There are "good" and "bad" deaths. With a good death, there is no loneliness, no suffering, no panic, no fear; it is peaceful; one simply goes to sleep. A bad death can be an extremely difficult experience for the patient and for caregivers in attendance, depending on circumstances. A bad death is accompanied by pain and suffering, loneliness, panic, or even fear, but most importantly, it has no accompanying peace. Many atheists claim a peaceful attitude toward life's end.

Sleep and death

Falling asleep is for me as close to blissfulness as any experience can be. Might death bring similar sensations, such peace? I suppose it depends on the surroundings, the setting, whether it is long in coming, and whether we have decided it is the way we want to die.

To die is not fair, but we must

At whatever age, we die for specific reasons. We develop diseases that kill us, we have accidents, and we are victims of violence. Some reasons are direct; some are indirect. Indirect reasons set us up for the fall. We either do not see them coming or choose to ignore them; therefore, the ultimate outcome comes sooner rather than later. Perhaps, because of our choices, we do not have the preferred time to prepare ourselves or others for death. It may be related to the disease process being far more advanced than initially thought. In these cases, days may make a difference. Time may run out. The patient may be too weak and the pathologic process advanced too far. Thus, the situation robs him or her of the reserve to recover and make it to treatment. In such a case, it is inevitable that the patient dies sooner than hoped and anticipated.

Last minute catch-up/last quarter rally may not work

Death will not be ignored or denied. Death is not a frightening monster, but it may occur unexpectedly, catching one by surprise if one does not prepare and observe. Listening to patients bargaining—gambling with life—is frustrating, for without planning, disease is often allowed to progress beyond the point of no return. Therefore, hope for extending life is lost because of the resulting unnecessary delays. Detecting changes as warning signs may provide opportunities for action.

Age makes a difference

As we age, losses and death—even simply reading about them—take on new meaning. Because we are then closer to death ourselves, we are affected more personally. It affects our thinking and may affect our choices from the point of that realization forward.

Slow death versus sudden death

Natural death is a commonly noted cause of death, but what does it mean? It depends on the circumstances, for it is natural to drop dead of a heart attack, and it is natural to die of a gunshot wound if you are the perpetrator of the crime or the crime fighter. The risk of accident, adverse reaction, and sudden death are greater possibilities than we realize as we go about our daily routines or have minor, much less major, medical procedures.

Slow death is usually of natural causes from some chronic disease, whatever the causal agent: chronic lung disease, hypertension, coronary heart disease, diabetes mellitus, or cancer.

Sudden death comes quickly. Sudden death is shocking. It takes us all by surprise. The final event!

"Hurry, begin CPR."

Even though there may be signs it is coming, the awesome abruptness is overwhelming. Life, as we have known and lived, is done.

The outcome may be the same whether warning signs are responded to or not. Prompt action with an urgent call to 911 is always appropriate. It is done with the hope that quick attention and emergency treatment will save a life.

Reactions from family survivors and friends to sudden death are acute, for it is a shock. They exclaim, "I can't believe this," "What happened?" "Do something." With chronic, slow death, the patient may have requested not to be resuscitated, and the process is more peaceful and the expectations temper acute reactions.

We lived our best with the tools we had

Dying over time is slower and is often a consequence of a chronic condition—one brought on by chance or from our environment, often a result of our own choices. Many have said, "If I'd known how much trouble being chronically ill is, I would've spent more time in my youth taking better care of myself." Wellness takes work. Serious illness, a life-and-death matter, makes us dependent on others. The whole process is long and arduous, filled with tough adjustments.

Chronic illness is weighted by a different tone, for you can "see" it coming, because it occurs at a snail's pace and over many years. This is manifested by normal aging with a slowdown in activities, fewer efforts to strive harder to get up and go and to eat, and by the need for more rest. There is a loss of the positive sense to take care toward recovery and wellness. In only a short time, individuals can begin the spiral into further deterioration. We ask, "Did they simply give up? Did their frustrations exasperate and exhaust them? Were they so depressed they gave up, or was the disease burden so great they couldn't overcome? In their effort, they lost appetite and weight, couldn't sleep, and were too tired to function normally. They were caught in a downward spiral that led to a hovering failure to thrive. Were they so sick they simply let go of the fight for survival?" There is no simple answer.

Patients and families first respond by thinking, "More can be done," and we want to see a turnaround. More action is an obligation in order to alleviate the downward spiral unless the patient and family step up to question the plan and feasibility for recovery. It is encouraging that a degree of reversal, or at least stability of the disease, is often possible. Those of us in the medical world encourage declaration of preference for action to pursue or not to pursue survival and recovery with a living will on admission to the hospital. We, as patients, continue to need the medical staff to advocate for and guide us.

Eventually, we follow our loved one's lead. Once we are convinced his or her can-do spirit has been expended, we elect temporary stability for the time being and begin thoughts and plans for what the future holds; we finally see these as his or her final days.

How to deal with the loss that comes ever so slowly

We usually understand the possible myriad of implications but do not see it as that. We would rather ask, what now? And then we enter the usual stages, from denial to acceptance. The initial denial may, in fact, function to keep us on our feet and moving forward. We often rationalize. Always put our best foot forward.

Take the example of this unique lady. The yield just was not great enough, as we say, at her age. It's not that she chose death in her mind. She only chose to avoid the misery of chemo for the brief benefit it would bring. She did not simply give up and die. She had a stent placed in the common bile duct to prevent the expanding pancreatic tumor from obstructing the duct, which would cause unnecessary suffering. Her decision to accept death from the tumor and avoid the misery of chemo was a tough one, but it allowed her to focus on "living" until the end. She was ninety-three years old with a life-ending cancer, and she decided not to put herself through chemotherapy.

She appeared calm, and if watched, she would stare off in the distance, perhaps toward her future life or reminiscing about her long life. She was calmer than anybody. She was quoted to say, "I'm not afraid. I'm ninety-three. When you're ninety-three, you're going to die of something. I knew something was going to get me. I don't have anything left to do."

Delaying the slow death

Dying is dying; why impose the label of slow death? Isn't it enough to call it chronic illness with all its implications? We must remember that all of the major illnesses/diseases have implied risks of death, even before they are clinically detected. Heart failure, for example, has been quoted as carrying a five-year survival time frame—that is, if treatment guidelines are not implemented. At that point, the chance for survival is not good. These guidelines are carried over to patient education and management. When they follow the guidelines, many people with differing forms of heart failure do well and live far longer than such predictions. Living longer does require work for all involved.

Cases involving sudden death

(1) She woke up hurting. This pain was different from her usual heart pain. She had a history of coronary artery bypass graft surgery and had received a coronary stent four months ago.

She was initially stable, but during the run to the emergency room, she suddenly soured when her heartbeat became erratic. The rescue team was far enough away from the hospital of choice, so they stopped the truck. Then, the two EMTs could more efficiently work the resuscitation; they even called for backup, but it did not help. They diverted to the nearest hospital, where the resuscitative efforts continued to no avail. Bettie died.

Ed witnessed it all. He had called 911 and followed the EMTs in his car. He was present when she died. All the events happened so quickly. He had depended on her all these years; all he could do was grieve.

(2) One friend had coronary artery disease and experienced unusual chest pain. He had an abnormal stress test, and his cardiologist recommended a coronary angiogram and, if needed, a coronary stent. He decided he wanted to wait because the conservative approach with delay was more comfortable for him and had given him success during his career. Soon thereafter, he discovered lumps in his neck, and a biopsy showed head and neck cancer. He was a smoker. Putting the two together and without involving his wife, he decided to do nothing and defended his decision. In a few months, he died suddenly while napping, waiting for his son to visit. His death was presumed to be caused by cardiac arrest. It seems as though that was a loss that could have been avoided. Sudden death has a way of winning out, for you can no longer question the person's decisions. Somehow, as devastating as his death was to his wife and son, they chose to see good in the suddenness of his death—as some rationalization that his decision was the right one. Therefore, they were OK.

(3) There was another patient who collapsed at home that was successfully resuscitated and lived. The resuscitative efforts were prolonged, including time in the field and in the emergency department of an outlying hospital. He required multiple shocks and intubation. Because he was critically ill, he was too unstable for transfer. Fortunately, I was familiar with those attending physicians and kept in touch with them and his family.

The good news is that he passed through the designation of sudden death to one of more chronic illness, where he had been in stable condition before the crisis. So now he resumed his slow-death status. The problem was the cardiac arrhythmia that caused his cardiac arrest (he momentarily died and was fortunate to be among the minority to live through the experience). He had pneumonia caused by aspiration when in acute arrest, and it improved. He was extubated. He underwent heart catheterization. His coronary angiogram showed stable coronary arteries. It was thought his arrhythmia (unstable heart rhythm) was related to scar tissue from the chronic disease—coronary heart disease. As he continued to improve, a defibrillator was implanted for protection from deadly heart rhythms. He was then discharged to rehab for a short stay before going home. Within ten days, I saw him back in the office in follow-up, and he was already his old, familiar self—what a guy!

(4) Bill was a friend who was hospitalized because he was dying from pancreatic cancer, diagnosed three months previously. Prior to that, he had enjoyed good health that was interrupted by abdominal pains. It took months and multiple CT scans to make the diagnosis. He was now comatose and had been so for days. I had read about and experienced an occasional patient waking up just before death. While making rounds before dawn one morning, I was surprised to find him wide-awake and alert. I called his wife, alerting her to come in for this last visit. Miraculously, they shared three hours after her arrival before he died. They needed this special time together to prepare each of them for his death and as closure for her. They reaffirmed their love, he thanked her for the life they had had together and apologized for his wrongdoings, and then they shared their goodbyes.

Did these people get the most out of living? No. For each of them, vibrant life was interrupted in midstep. (1) The first (husband) found no peace and continues to grieve. (2) The second (wife) felt a sense of peace, for her husband had died as he had lived—without including her in his decisions. (3) The third (wife) was kept informed, was the decision maker, and found both closure and peace in her husband's recovery. (4) The fourth (couple) found peace, as best they could, in their goodbyes. All survivors are now aware of the value of life and the importance of living each moment as if it were their last. We will not know, though, whether the subject of the second example was planning a special visit with his son and was preparing by taking a rest.

We can never be sure when saying goodbye or taking a breath whether it will be our last. Therefore, we had best take advantage of each new day and every opportunity to help ourselves and those we leave behind find peace in death, as we part.

6
HOSPICE AND PALLIATIVE CARE: THE DETAILS OF DYING

"SINCE WE HAVE EXPENDED ENERGY DURING OUR LIVES TO BE DIGNIFIED, OF GOOD CHARACTER AND THOUGHTFUL OF OTHERS, WE DESERVE TO DIE THAT WAY: TAKEN CARE OF BY OTHERS WITH GENTLENESS, DIGNITY AND RESPECT, ESPECIALLY WHEN WE'RE NOT ABLE TO CARE FOR OURSELVES.
—*Anonymous*

Final preparations for the care of the seriously ill

Candidates for consultation with a palliative-care service organization are people with serious illness; those with multiple, chronic, potentially serious diseases that need close management; those who are incapable of caring for themselves; those who have little or no support; and those who are not dying but have been told they only have a short life left.

Palliative Care

Palliative care is as complete as necessary to provide quality of life through support and coordinated, holistic means to relieve pain and other symptoms for those who have serious illnesses. It is a multidisciplinary medical specialty and is designed to support all the needs of the patient and family, including emotional, physical, and spiritual needs and goals. They work with the primary medical team in the treatment of the individual in the home setting.

It is advisable to seek palliative care assistance early in the illness to alleviate suffering and improve life's quality. Controlling physical pain and providing needed support earlier provides significant benefits. It offers comfort, reduces depression, minimizes the perception of loneliness through caring support, and even prolongs survival. If more comfortable, the patient can better manage his or her attitude in favor of care and toward others. Palliative care is provided in concert with conventional care, with combined goals for recovery and return to better health.

Delce decided she had been tired long enough, so she finally came in for the needed evaluation. She was found to have suffered a silent heart attack with risk factors of smoking, hypertension, high cholesterol, and diabetes. No wonder she felt fatigued; these issues were not going away, and they would predictably worsen. She went on to have a coronary angiogram, resulting in two stents. She was, of course, overwhelmed with so much chronic disease and the need to take so many medications and to follow up with so many doctors. Part of her surprise was because so much disease was present in an advanced form at discovery, and she was one who thought she knew her body well and was able to keep up with it. She didn't know what to do.

She needed coaching. She never realized that palliative care services could focus on the chronically ill. It seemed that palliative care offered more support. The nurse assured Delce that she wasn't dying soon, and that she could envision herself with the potential for improvement and the ability to return to her energetic self, able to enjoy full activities and feel well again.

That palliative care prolongs life was reported in a 2010 study published in the *New England Journal of Medicine*. The lead author of the article was Dr. Jennifer S. Temel, an oncologist at Massachusetts General Hospital. The study confirmed that providing early palliative care to a group of cancer patients resulted in a better quality of life, fewer symptoms of depression, and longer life than patients who received only traditional oncology care.

When symptoms arise, patients need to respond quickly so valuable time for evaluation and treatment is not lost. To be unaware that we have a chronic illness and are essentially dying slowly will be a loss. If dying, we want to know the disease status and obtain help to manage it so life can be optimized. This is a goal most families pursue. As long as loved ones live, it is best to do everything possible to stay informed and advocate optimizing health. Palliative support services will assist us, and our physician as he or she cares for us. As we are better supported and cared for, we will be able to think of those we leave behind and include them as we both live and die.

End of life

The end-of-life care of the very sick and terminally ill is a growing field. These cases commonly originate from chronic illnesses that progress over time until the disease burden is beyond reversal. After appropriate discussions with the patients and their families, these situations call for shifting from prevention of disease and preservation of health to survival and salvage and discussions to prepare for death.

Hospice care

Hospice services are an option for the terminally ill whose survival is usually no more than six months. This is a program for end-of-life care that offers comfort and support to patients and families similar to that offered by palliative care programs. Hospice patients require other than the usual medical care. These programs focus on the highest possible quality of life until the last breath. If the care is needed past the six months, it continues. The staff is trained and experienced in providing services for the full spectrum of medical diseases that have reached incurable stages. These services can often be provided in the home or an in-patient setting.

We have discussed sudden death and slow death associated with chronic illness. There is death that is as good as it gets and death that is to be avoided because it is unpleasant for all involved. The former death comes after proper preparations, whereas unpleasant death is associated with greater uncertainties, pain and suffering, and chaos in support. The latter are to be avoided. Calling on hospice is not an act of giving up. It's giving in to a support system that works, allowing those who are experienced in symptom management to help us. Receiving guidance so we can best live out our lives is all we can control. Hospice organizations are known for helping families through their support services.

Hastening death—aid in dying

Even though we are taught that death is an enemy, it is considered and even welcomed when life is depleted. Assisted death has, to date, been seen with disfavor and resisted. Assisted suicide or doctor-assisted suicide is a topic that includes medical, psychiatric, moral, ethical, philosophical, and societal issues. Currently, it is illegal in most of the United States. Thus far, the only organization that provides recommendations for aid in dying is the American Public Health Association, and the states that support this practice limit the right to mentally competent adults who are terminally ill. The data from early experiences indicate this group of patients, as a whole, are more educated.

Hastening death takes thought, for the more we allow it, the greater the fear that it will be overutilized and include persons whose situations might best be managed otherwise. The assumption is that in considering hastened death, the patients are those at life's end due to degenerative or metastatic disease with inordinate, mortal pain and suffering and lack of resources, who have lost their will to live and are desperate to die. Each case is unique and individual, but all seem to be filled with tragedy and lack of support. These persons come from all walks of life; the scenarios seem endless.

How much of the ongoing trauma of the major events suffered by these people leads to major depression, extreme anxiety, and posttraumatic stress syndrome, each and all capable of clouding any picture? What are the effects of these and other preexisting psychological problems? What is related to the primary and comorbid diseases, and what is the effect of any illegal drug use and drugs used in treatment—chemo, psychotropics, and other therapies? And what if the decision to assist in dying takes too long and the pain, trauma, and suffering accentuates the subtle-to-gross changes from competence to incompetence? At what point would the establishment recognize the change and still allow the aid in dying to proceed?

These persons, whether competent or not, are ideal candidates for hospice, where these myriad issues might best be sorted out for optimal decision and management. Of course, each candidate needs a personal advocate to accompany or represent him or her. Managed death is a process in evolution. We may need to more broadly face this management dilemma as we continue to explore the brain and its functional responses related to the body, especially when at the abyss with the terminally ill—at life's very end.

Share details of preference for your care. You are the mentor, the family role model.

Living wills are useful in general terms as we and our families contemplate the what-ifs, especially when recovering after illness or hospitalizations. The questions for us to instill in those caring for us is where we want to die—in the hospital, or, if we have a choice, at home. Consider allocating someone you think understands your wishes and best interests to be the durable power of attorney for your health matters, to assume your decisions. Another general concept represented in the living will is how far we want our care providers to go to keep us alive.

Advanced directives and living wills

By discussing death, we are not rushing toward it. Discussing it does not make it happen sooner. By addressing it, we can remove some of the tensions surrounding death and adjust our thoughts and those of our family members so we can live better, happier, and healthier lives knowing what to anticipate when that inevitable time comes. Preparing for a good death can begin a positive process for change. Yes, it may seem uncomfortable now, but it will be less so for all when it does happen if preparations have been made.

It may be helpful to cite examples of advanced directives and living wills. The intention is to keep it simple and to ensure your wishes are as clear as possible. The challenge is to convey the essence of your wishes so that as the details of the various scenarios change, your wishes still have relevance.

The forms for living will/advanced directives ask you questions for desired care in the event you are not expected to recover. The specific terminology includes: "terminal condition," "in a coma with no reasonable expectation of regaining consciousness," or "in a persistent vegetative state with no reasonable expectation of regaining significant cognitive function." Most of us can expect not to desire prolonged care for such a state, especially if we then have negative expectations about our health, feel bad presently, and lack long-term projections for the "full" life. See example form in Appendix B.

The settings

The questions about what is to be done do not begin when one enters the door for a medical procedure. Answers are not to be given from impulse. Surely, the thought process best begins many years sooner.

The impact of influence

These issues begin when we are young and healthy. When young, we see ourselves as invincible, which is a normal and healthy view, and a positive attitude to have. However, this is a form of normal denial. I have said in the past, "I have a hernia, and it hurts. You recommend surgery. OK, let's set the date." And that assumes the surgeon explained the method and risks of surgery and recovery to me, gave educational pamphlets to me, and outlined appropriate timelines.

Ignoring obvious signs alerting one to a health problem, however, is abnormal behavior. How many times did encounters in our past influence us to react in an unhealthy manner today? Were we able to separate ourselves from the impact of childhood memories when our siblings, parents, grandparents, and others were so sick? Do we adopt our elders' uncertainty and fears about illness and death? Do we adopt some of their resistance and their complaints about seeking, receiving, and adapting to recommendations from the medical profession? Is this an issue of trust, influenced from the past, or do we presently trust with difficulty anyway? Such lessons can give us the basis for our attitudes and response patterns unless we rethink them and decide to be different.

As an example, a sixty-seven-year-old man with severe vascular disease affecting his ability to walk needed to have surgery. His history reported he was a long-term, heavy smoker who was not interested in stopping, even when told his habit was accentuating the disease process. The anticipated procedure had proven to give excellent results in restoring circulation. After he was informed of all the details, his preference was to avoid surgery and recovery hassles; he did not want to suffer. That called for more education to inform him of the ravages from suffering in store for him later, when his leg circulation and perhaps his health in general worsened. His resistance persisted. It was discouraging to hear that his wife reinforced his preferences. After talking further, it was evident that his attitude originated from his past. He insisted he was acting out of his own free will. But was he? At that time we didn't pursue the origin of his resistant attitude further. We might have questioned whether he was the youngest child or had been influenced by his elders during their hard times. His response may well represent the way he has lived. Unless he changes, his past predicts the remainder of his life with complications, unwanted misery, and early death.

The complexity of these issues and their origins can be confusing. We are definitely influenced by others. The memories may be blocked by the pain of the original incidences. The loss felt, but not expressed, lingers in one's memory, is retained over a lifetime, and is waiting to have influence later when catastrophe hits.

Our families have their eyes on us

Picture your family watching you, for they are. Your family members, those who love you and think you're worth having around, are observing you and your actions. Look into their eyes. Surely, you see their concern for you. You are not alone with that energy and force behind you. As you take care of yourself, it is OK to ask questions, which are useful tools for you as you process these health questions and learn how to assist yourself through your evaluation and efforts to get well. You need to understand what is to be done and given an opportunity to ask your questions and to be given comfort in order to make decisions and proceed.

Example cases that risk a catastrophic medical life-threatening event, not end-of-life issues—the benefits of thinking about and discussing care

Let's look at a few case scenarios. Most of these examples are not end-of-life issues, but occasionally complications occur that change the scenario. The next and more specific step is to use this process to talk in more detail with your family and doctors at the appropriate time. The purpose is to be informed.

1) A twenty-four-year-old healthy adult with too numerous insect stings—yellow jackets, bees, or fire ants—with delay in getting help because of location and now developing dizziness and trouble breathing. There's no EpiPen available. Someone finally called 911.

2) A sixty-five-year-old, apparently healthy lady with no need for doctor visits in two years presents to the emergency department with a two-day history of abdominal pain over the appendix area, worsened severely in the last two hours, with dehydration and lots of abnormal lab results. She may become extremely sick if her appendix is ruptured. Will she develop complications? She's in the right place for emergent assessment and a visit with the surgeon, even if her symptoms are caused by a viral illness or food poisoning.

3) A sixty-eight-year-old lady with hypertension and two days of headache presents with speech difficulty and is coughing and unable to move her dominant right extremities. She suddenly loses consciousness as EMTs bring her into the emergency department. Something serious is going on, and she must be assessed and attended to quickly.

We are not able to choose the scenario in which we want to be a part. With each case, time is of the essence. The solution for each is similar, for in these examples, all but the stroke victim may survive with few residual problems, but significant risks for each are present. Such a prediction has to be borne out by paying attention to details and providing expert service in a timely manner. The stroke victim's outcome depends on the severity of the brain damage, what areas are involved, the effectiveness of the acute stroke unit's rapid response, and close monitoring of acute care. Availability of the best and latest treatment protocol or quick transfer to a facility specifically developed to quickly handle these cases, when appropriate, is essential.

Risks vary. Whether being put under general anesthesia or not, having an acute problem (see examples), experiencing an exacerbation of a chronic problem, having a procedure, or being taken to a rural or an urban facility, the patient is experiencing an acute life-threatening event, and each detail is a factor. The risk is also compounded by who is administering care, how much sleep the doctor and staff had lost, and whether the patient has been given medications, had any procedures, or required interventions. Each can make a difference. Therefore, the details require discussion, even when the patient insists that he or she understands.

What do you want done when unexpected complications occur?

It is reasonable to expect the team to attend to each person by correctly evaluating and treating the problem. Elderly people usually have acquired risk factors that are, hopefully, controlled. Any justified procedure done is to relieve pain and improve health, if not to save a life.

What do you want done when catastrophe hits, your heart stops, or you can't breathe: end-of-life issues?

This takes clarification. A person needs reassurance that she or he will be taken care of. We are exposed to a number of folks who are either confused by their pasts and experiences or simply do not understand the different issues being discussed. It's also easy for the manly type to say, "I want to die quickly with my boots on." That is impossible to compute, for we usually do not have such a choice. It only appears by chance.

If a patient happens to lapse into unconsciousness with a good chance of recovery, then she or he should opt for the full-resuscitation/full-code. If improvement during the first few days is slow, it is time to reevaluate the status and decide whether to continue an aggressive approach. If progress is positive, continue maximal efforts and repeat the process after two more days. If at that time the patient has deteriorated or improved, the change is usually clear and decisions can be made. Maybe the person has awakened and can give his or her opinion.

It is best to talk beforehand about what to expect and to clearly say that this is the time to do everything possible, for conquering these challenges and continuing living are the primary goals. It might be useful to discuss methods of communication in the event the person is intubated for a brief time. Thankfully, he or she will be sedated until just before the tube is removed, when the medical team will inform the person what their intentions and plans are. The staff will talk the patient through the process.

An ordinary lady

Janet asked me, "Am I doing the right thing?" She had chosen hospice care, for she did not want to keep living like this. She decided to no longer submit herself to vigorous, aggressive treatment for her chronic heart failure and recurring rapid heartbeat. She did want her associated anxiety and fears treated. I assumed she knew the answer to her question and that I did not need to answer directly, so I simply sat on her bed and held her hand. She cried. After she calmed, she asked for a hug, and we said our goodbyes. All the people supporting her were present, and arrangements had been made to transfer her to the in-patient center for hospice patients that afternoon.

Janet was a bright, youthful, mentally clear eighty-six-year-old lady I met after she was admitted two years previously with acute congestive heart failure. Her failure was aggravated by a rapid heartbeat, too fast to sustain normal heart pump function. She had an underlying weakened heart due to these uncontrolled, recurring arrhythmias prior to my introduction to her case. Her primary care physician had previously treated her for recurring anxiety. It is known that anxiety can be a natural result of heart failure because of the chemicals produced with each occurrence. She had suffered admission frequency of every two to three months. She was miserable and suffering through each admission. Regular management and follow-up by me, her primary care physician, and the heart-failure clinic, though helpful, did not change her ultimate course.

She had been her husband's caregiver for six years before he died four years previously and was still grieving. In spite of her grief and illnesses, two months prior to her decision to transfer to hospice, I ran into her in Michaels, where she was buying craft supplies needed to display flowers "to make the house more livable." She was a delight, though appalled she wasn't dressed and made up properly to see me. Overall, at times during those few years, we enjoyed occasional long talks. I had a sense there was much more to her than her diseases.

We had accepted the challenge of closely attending to her heart with frequent visits and optimal use of the medications until we were convinced it was her severe and failing heart, and not her compliance with all our rules, that prevented her from improving. She was obviously not a candidate for a heart-assist device operation or heart-transplant surgery. She was dying with end-stage heart disease. We read of her death three weeks later. The obituary let us in on her life story, which put a lot of pieces of the puzzle together. A good death for a classy lady.

These things don't just happen to regular folks, for it happened to a famous heart surgeon too: his story

I heard the story of Dr. Michael DeBakey, who at age ninety-seven suffered chest pains that sent him to the hospital where he had spent his career as a cardio-thoracic surgeon. The team diagnosed a split in the aorta in his chest—an aortic dissection. The treatment was surgery, but he was resistant to proceed. Over a short while, he deteriorated to the point of requiring a ventilator. Then his labs showed signs of multiorgan failure. He became unresponsive, and death was imminent. He had completed a living will that explicitly forbade heroic measures, for, I suppose, at his age, his thoughts were to let himself die.

As the story goes, in a cloud of controversy, his wife demanded that the hospital board overrule the directions given in the living will and find a surgeon and anesthesiologist to perform the life-saving surgery. Incidentally, the surgical procedure used had previously been developed by Dr. DeBakey. He had the surgery, and after a long and complicated in-hospital stay, coupled with rehab, recovered back to good health. When later asked about the preferences in the living will, he is reported to have said, "Oh, I didn't mean that." More than once, he was heard expressing gratitude to the team for deciding to go ahead with the surgery.

The question for Dr. DeBakey then, and for us now, is, did he and his wife discuss the true meaning of the question and the consequences involved? Did he think from his perspective alone? Did she perform her heroic act because she knew that he was strong and that the team would get him through all he needed to endure? This story reinforces the importance of taking the time to discuss the topic in detail, for these are, indeed, life-and-death matters.

7
GRIEVING AND MOURNING

Many individuals are judged to overrestrain fun and enjoyment for a prolonged period of time after the death of a loved one (see chapter one). Is guilt at play here? It's difficult to avoid enjoyment unless one stops "living." Is this practice done in the name of the loved one? Is this behavior for the benefit of others? What would the deceased spouse think? What were his or her wishes for you, the real ones meaningful to both of you?

Grief is defined as great sadness or intense, deep, and profound sorrow. Its manifestations depend on individual, ethnic, and cultural factors. Its appearance varies from a quiet, staid response to a lively and emotional reaction.

For now, your goal is to live, to get through life. It is as though you have been hit by a truck and have a long way to go before you can be on your own two feet and sensible again. If you smile or spontaneously enjoy something, you are not desecrating bonds shared with your loved one. He or she would understand what you are going through and where you are right now.

Grief can be sudden, shocking, and devastating. It can be worse because we did not grieve before, when we stored up the emotions of loss. It comes from loss of close attachments here and there. All of a sudden, someone we're not so close to dies; then, out of the blue, we cannot stop clearing our throat, we cry at a sensitive moment in a movie, or wham, we are emotionally affected and wonder why.

Grief over losses—your job, a sudden devastating illness from which you recover, the death of a close friend, the simultaneous deaths of multiple friends, the damage or loss of your house by fire or storm, the theft of sentimental jewelry, or the death of a dog you love—these things are gone, and it is your loss. I would never be so crass as to think that the loss of an inanimate object would equal the loss of a person, for it will not. But it may be the surrounding history involving a person close to you involved in a traumatic event that triggers the reaction, which is deeper than you could imagine. The accumulation of a number of events can be sufficient trauma to affect coping mechanisms and aggravate the grief. The loss of the object may trigger reactions associated with attachments to meaningful persons in your life that have been hidden for years.

Grieving after the loss of a child is known as loss of the highest order, followed by loss of a spouse, another family member, or a close life-long friend.

Grief comes in stages:
1. Denial/isolation/disbelief/shock
2. Pain/guilt
3. Anger/bargaining
4. Sadness/depression/fear/anxiety/panic
5. Hope/acceptance

Life goes on with or without us. We have experienced the seemingly uncaring world when in our sorrow. There certainly is a struggle during and following the loss, and then a challenge to go on—to keep moving forward when challenged, when older, when sick, and when grieving.

Maintenance and survival

Maintenance is one thing, survival another. Placing one foot in front of the other, going forward—how does one do it? Obviously, you have to be still, sit and think, talk, cry, and complain, alone and with others—all when you are ready. There are immediate needs, some of which you have planned for, and here's hoping you are fortunate to have someone there who is willing to help, for you need help to focus and stay on track. It's OK to make time to do those necessary, busy things. It's OK to plan times to mope and to cry on a regular basis. Maintenance is just that—maintaining you, doing only those things that are necessary to get through the funeral and to chalk off the top items on your someone-has-died to-do list.

Survival dictates you need more help from others than you anticipated, for you are broken. You are struggling daily to make it, uninterested in taking care of usual hygienic activities or eating, no longer eager to get out of bed, and wondering how to continue. Usually, and thankfully, someone steps up, ready to assist you. And they do, in spite of resistance.

Salvage represents your worst state of brokenness. Are you sick and so damaged that you have given up and are focusing on death for yourself? Death is inevitable, but this is not the proper time to contemplate that. Are you drowning in your sorrow? Do you need more time? Are you rational? Are you thinking clearly? Should others call for professional help, possibly to treat depression? Are you lonely and depressed? Is that what your precious love would want? He or she knew it would be tough for you, but not necessarily this bad. Sounds as if you need help and need to talk. Please consider seeing your physician to discuss your situation; your need for medications for the stress, anxiety, sleep deprivation, and depression; and how to improve your coping capacity.

You need more time.

Prolonged grief and sorrow rob one of living

Things to watch or listen for:
- the fear of being stuck and unable to live life to the fullest and love anything again
- the fear and fact of not sleeping, of panicking, of being depressed, and of obsessive busyness
- the fear that you can't live again, potentially the greatest loss

Don't waste your days. Get help.

Grief

- Grief is a sad situation.
- After previous losses, has your sadness gotten progressively worse?
- Was your loved one disadvantaged or mistreated early in life?
- Did it affect the way she or he lived?
- Did his or her behavior affect others?
- You know the history, saw the impact, and feel saddened.

- Your experiences and sufferings to date contribute to who you are, how you react, and how you live.
- These sufferings eventually fade and are left behind. But they have further shaped you—reinforcing, building, or diminishing you, preparing you for what lies ahead.

- Your experiences will change you.
- We each have a world view, how we receive/react to change.
- The world changes, and we change with it.

- These are issues of choice.
- Your response will be improved or not, depending on your choice.
- Keep choice in mind, and choose wisely.
- With the chafe and friction of life will come doubts and questions.

- It's OK to doubt, challenge your thinking, and ask questions, including those about your beliefs.

Changes outside of us are associated with adaptation and helps one to change too, to cope. Then you can continue in the struggle to place one foot in front of the other. It seems this misery will last forever. You can tell yourself, "But with time, I will reach the other side. And, with time, I'll be left with all my memories. Yes, I remember the bliss, the talks, the walks, and the fun. I can do this; I will keep walking."

What to do?

The goal at hand depends on whether one is contemplating future death, facing serious illness and impending death, or dying, or if one is the caregiver and facing the death of a loved one. Dying brings the need to complete legal and financial documents, to reflect on legacy; dying connects one with the business of death and the many arrangements needed. Most of us need guidance, especially when grieving. There are many items to think of.

To-do list
—Think about what you want.
—Include your spouse.
—Include your family.
—Write it down.
—Make plans.
—Consider talking with others: your doctor and friends.
—Consider the children.
—Live in the moment.

Before death

The story of what Jeffrey did for himself

Jeffrey M. Piehler wrote an opinion piece for the *New York Times* that was published Feb. 1, 2014 and titled "Ashes to Ashes, but

First a Nice Pine Box." This is a fascinating, self-examining, and exposing description with a clear explanation of his journey. He is a retired doctor with terminal cancer who is relatively stable and interested in building his own coffin. He got the idea after attending a young person's funeral. The boy was to be cremated in a fancy, expensive box. Piehler wanted his to be simpler and less expensive; thus, the pine box. His story is emotionally moving.

He was assisted in building the box by someone he initially would not have paired with, which is a story in itself. They bonded and became friends and had meaningful discussions. The other story involved his family's sentiments too—a story of spiritual growth. They finally calmed their shock as to his intentions, realized he wasn't crazy, and appreciated his willingness to take on this project to completion and celebrate.

To quote, "The project has smoothed the rough edges of my thoughts. It's pretty much impossible to feel anger at someone for driving too slowly in front of you in traffic when you've just come from sanding your own coffin. Coveting material objects, holding on to old grudges, failing to pause and see the grace in strangers—all equally foolish. While the coffin is indeed a reminder of what awaits us all, its true message is to live every moment to its greatest potential." Dr. Piehler truly has the healthy image and framework for living. He is freeing himself, mind and body, of unnecessary and unwanted residual angst and negative reactions that bind each of us. He is living the full life and will eventually die while enjoying the same, a goal for all.

Through his activities with family and friends and building the coffin, he initiated celebration. He is on track to continue it until the end. He has grown, changed, and become more human through his experiences with cancer. This project has elevated him to a new place in life—he has ownership. Through his article, he was clearly thankful and intended to continue his celebration of life for all to partake in and enjoy.

Prepare—it's time to celebrate; begin the process now

What we each need to do now is to get with family and friends as often as desired and begin our celebration of Life! One lives the full life by enjoying the company and fellowship of friends and family. This allows community to thrive. It opens communications so stale differences from unpleasant memories with attached negative feelings from the past will dissipate in the renewed connections. Otherwise, we stay with the status quo—in more of a broken state than acknowledged—do not brighten the light, do not connect. If negative feelings are retained, the overall struggle will cause loneliness that fosters negative energy and accentuates disease processes.

So, the first thing to do is to have a get-together. Why force your family and friends to talk about you with old memories when they can be with and enjoy you now? And, of course, it works both ways—this is not a race to the end, but who's to say who will go first? The important thing is to act and avoid further delay, for time is of the essence. Parties can be tiring, but encourage getting together and let others do the work, keeping the costs low and the hours reasonable. When you are lying in a box, you cannot take part, and the opportunity is lost. By celebrating often before it's too late, you will be extending the fulfillment we all desire.

Grief is necessary and important

Before the event and when in a less sad and melancholic mood, follow your head, talk with your loved one, and consider writing a list of important things you'll need to do with time lines: include times to be done in days, weeks, months, or years. This may precondition you and provide alerts when things need to be done when you're less inclined to act. You may engage others among family, friends, or legal folks to help you get things done. Keep the to-do list at hand and refer to it from time to time to catch any deadlines that may be approaching. Consider beginning the process now.

There is a relatively healthy, eight-eight-year-old man who was forced to retire at eighty-four, and he is still not accepting the reality of it. His wife suffers with progressive Alzheimer's disease. Her dementia is severe, and at times she does not even know him. Of course, it's tough for him, for he, as a rational thinker, continually tries to reason with her. She's not amenable to reason, yet he forgets. The stress is surfacing in his own age-related problems with elevated blood pressure and less clarity of his thinking. He's beginning to slip at times. He clearly needs all the help and encouragement we can give him.

He's preached the Gospel each visit to anyone who will listen and actually presents himself and his topics in a way that draws listeners to him. For the many years I have known him and them as a couple, he has been a strong leader. He notes he is beginning to doubt his beliefs and God's purpose because of the inhumane nature of the rapid and devastating disease affecting his wife. He's finally hit an obstacle in life he cannot jump over or walk around and feels defeated and abandoned. He agrees that it takes the hard issues to fine-tune us. The loss of his relationship with his wife is a sad one and could potentially break him. He noted that it would be easier if she died than for both of them to suffer so. I predict he will get through this based on his solid faith and the support of his daughters and many friends, those who appreciate his efforts and have known the both of them. Hopefully, his frailty showing through his strong nature, manifested by an unkempt appearance; recent forgetfulness, and lost and melancholic feelings, are signs of bubbling grief that he will work through. We will continue to follow the both of them.

After death

Sometimes we lag behind, caught in the grip

The grip of grief is influenced by personal attachments to the person, both the positive and negative encounters. Both negatives, guilt and regret—forms of loss from previous encounters—continue to have impact, for they were left unresolved.

What makes us walk and live as if walking backward? It may be because we focus on the past, on our perceived mistakes and regrets or our guilt and questions about whether we did enough or our best. There is something about the loss and the attachment that reinforces our feelings about the person, stemming from our history with him or her. Perhaps it is related to our dependence on them. Is it something in our pasts, from our childhood, associated with parenting? We drift back to our pasts.

All these events may suddenly hit one like a ton of bricks weeks and months later, and at that point, one is overwhelmed and suffering. This is where living and dying; sudden death versus slower, chronic-disease-associated death; palliation and hospice; and hope and love connect.

This is life—the parts we often avoid. Let's not avoid or fear them; let's embrace them as part of life. With these efforts, we will eventually turn around and go forward.

Gather all your support and often

After the death of your loved one, the loss is your loss. Hopefully, your children and family are your support, and friends will help fill in the gaps. If you've helped your children and family in their own education about what has happened and what is expected to happen from now forward, you can focus on yourself and allow them to support you until you get back on your feet. Since you are the survivor, there is nothing to divide, nothing to change. Though you have not died, you feel like it. You even feel lifeless. Let's assume you are overworked. Exhaustion is the norm. You need to rest, so do it.

Some may be more OK than you, but possibly you have been grieving as you toiled with your dying spouse for years. And the stress burden may be higher if he or she was stubborn and if he or she carried on without any thought of getting better or changing for better health. The experience may have frustrated, depressed, and prevented you from feeling fulfilled in the job you did; there still is something missing in you. You have great memories of wonderful moments together, but these last few years have been trying. So you will grieve and do it your own way. Surround yourself with people you want to be with and grieve as you go. Hopefully, your sense of self-satisfaction will be realized, or you will need to make it happen. You may have to grant it to yourself—you do deserve that claim—that you did your best and gave your all. Then, you can begin to focus on better times with fond memories that have been overshadowed in recent years.

I have observed occasional grievers in my own family to immediately begin home renovation projects after their spouses' deaths. These aberrations were obviously projects borne out of conflict. In one such case, it was, "He held me back. Now's time to catch up. I will be OK." And in this particular case, she was.

Mourning

Mourning is for the strong and the less strong. This does not include the weak, for strength is more a matter of response based on our hurts, fears, memories, and experiences that make us who we are. The greater loss, the death of a partner, affects our perceptions related to our hope. We need out hope. Hope that is not lost in the fog of grief enables us to forecast how well we will do, summon our resources for action, receive and reach out to others, and retake and reshape our lives going forward.

This means: It is OK to mourn, Mourn, Mourn, and follow your broken heart.

It is also OK for action.

Many in your situation have been observed and studied over time. Stages and stage durations have been charted, but there is no set time sequence to this process. It's OK to say, "For me, life goes on and may pass me by for now, but perhaps I will catch up later when I have the energy for it—if it returns." It is also OK to keep moving.

You may need help

Your loss is mammoth and similar to losing part of your own DNA. It takes a variable amount of time to traverse the shadow-filled valley. The past is important and more than history for some of you. You will usually proceed as you have lived. It is, however, hard—nearly impossible—to move on for some. It is OK to stay submerged in the past for a while, especially if one's thoughts are in honor of the loved one. It is also OK to think it through if not discussed previously. If, however, you are so dependent on that wonderful person that you are now absolutely lost, you do need help.

Did you discuss the inevitable and make plans? What were the instructions you each promised the other for life going forward from this point? If it was clear, you are still to give yourself more time, then focus on the assignment you agreed to. When ready, rewrite the instructions on paper, then expound on them in real-life terms to make them real for you. You might write down what you honor and what you miss the most. It will help to make a list of the memory highlights, both the good and the bad. They both may even seem silly once you think about them, or they may let you realize you miss your loved one because you did not tell him or her about hurts you did not appreciate at the time or that you did not say goodbye as you would have wished. You may find something comical about the experience. You may reread the obituary and contemplate the many positives that made your loved one who he or she was and appreciate the comfort.

Best to let some things go

If you were there with your continued presence and care and in the end saw to it that your loved one died in calmness and with peace, then you did your job. Let's assume that no one could have done a better job and that no one could have done more. You can feel great satisfaction with the loving service you gave. After you write down these thoughts and specific facts about the care given, you may realize that any lack of completeness and closure on your part is a head thing. Think on those facts. The feeling of lack of closure may come from your loss—you are lonely, and your loved one's absence looms. You wonder if there was something more you might have done that would have made a difference. Eventually, it will be best to let such thoughts go. You should find that the facts you wrote down would show that you made maximal efforts. Simply do not harbor them, for they will only burden you. Release them.

What's best now is to turn your back on the past and move away from it, for it only clouds your otherwise clear perception of the special relationship you had with your loved one. Such thoughts may interfere with the fact that you gave your best to her or him and that the relationship—your loved one's spirit—will live on in your mind and in your vivid memories for as long as you live.

In that, and with time, you can find peace. Herein lies hope in rekindling that flicker of life within you. Your experiences with your loved one have contributed to making you who you are. They will give you strength to sustain yourself and be content within your own skin and to find independence. These are some of the steps that will propel you forward to live life to the fullest as best you can. And the recovered you is tied to and in part, because of your strength in the relationship, with your departed.

It's OK to be energetic

With the strength, energy, and desire to continue your usual pace, take advantage of it and make the most of this time. This is a time for change and for doing something for yourself. Your determined busyness produces progress for you for now. You may resume something you enjoyed doing with your spouse in the past that made you both feel healthy and bonded, such as a running or other workout program, alone or with friends. After projects are completed, you may feel an energy lull that will require adjustments. So be aware.

What do I specifically do?

Teach your children

We as parents are our children's most influential teachers. Children will learn from your influence, even if they are adults. Their children will learn from you too. Especially in this sphere, we are to lead the way. What does that look like?

Plan
Plan
Plan
Rehearse
Repeat

Begin early. Extend the process to each generation until the ideas are rote. Make them part of the ritual of children's bedtime stories and prayers. The following childhood prayer will serve as a familiar example.

Now I lay me down to sleep,
I pray the Lord my soul to keep;
if I die before I wake,
I pray the Lord my soul to take.

This is the time to build in the ideas about the questions, what if I do die? How do I view it? Now? Yes, and later too.

Assure your children that you will be OK and will be there for them. You'll need to do crisis management for a while. If, in fact, you see them lagging or not rebounding here and there, their behavior may be keying off of yours because of your own reactions and feelings that need more focus. Your awareness of yourself and your willingness to listen to others' feedback will be assets in monitoring your overall situation. You may need to take time off to focus on yourself and the children. Reducing their stress is important, but you can only give to them if you are OK.

Teach your children that death is natural, expected, and not to be feared. That life is about relationships, beginning with family. That meaningful relationships are to be respected, embraced, nurtured, shared, and enjoyed. The sharing can bring learning experiences for them. Through these bonds, life will have meaning, and in their efforts, they will find purpose. They will learn the importance of the balance between relationships, family, working or career, play, and recreational activities. They will learn the basics of the full life and later realize the depth of your influence on them. You'll teach them the art and science of "living" and the importance of relationships.

Use of social media versus the written note for communication

Our young are growing up using social media. Their preferences and methods for communication are different from ours. Their expressions are relevant to their peers—persons of similar age. They tend to keep the interactions casual, without concern for privacy and confidentiality. The participants do not usually react meaningfully but have more of a matter-of-fact, self-centered approach, even with grief issues. It is best to remember that they will be brief and light, so expect it.

Live in the moment and write

Consider the value of looking within by looking beyond the self, using mindfulness, prayer, and meditation. Thinking is helpful if guided, talking is simple yet fleeting, but writing puts the thoughts into concrete form and is more helpful. At least begin with talking, for it may take talking to someone else to help let go the sting and pain. Writing in the third person first, then in first person, may nail thoughts down over time for review later. Often on reread, one finds evidence for change in thought tones over time, which is a sign of movement, or growth.

Give in and try it—work the project

Another thing to do, when appropriate, is to finally take up your long-term friend's plea to help with that project he or she has bugged you about over the last few years. Sure, it's doing something for others, and that may help you look beyond yourself and open up to what life has in store for you and your future. You may not like it, but it might provide the opportunity for you to develop your own ideas for something you would rather do. Or it may be the perfect shoe-fit, and you will dive in and enjoy it.

8
MANAGING LIFE'S JOURNEY: HEALTH AND AGING

"I HAVE SO MUCH LIVING AHEAD OF ME; IT SEEMS I'LL NEVER DIE.
I'M FREE TO LEARN, TO EXPLORE, AND TO PURSUE MY DREAMS."
—*The voice of youth*

"BUT, O FRIENDS, I DO NOT WANT TO DIE; I WANT
TO LIVE, IN ORDER TO THINK AND SUFFER."
—*Alexander Sergeyevich Pushkin, "Elegy," 1830*

Why the focus on the journey—health and aging?

Can anyone say he or she takes advantage of all that life has to offer without some reference to death? After all, it is a subject that is always with us. Death is evident in the media, worldwide and at home; on our streets; and in churches, synagogues, and mosques. It involves people we know and those we do not. It is an unspoken comparison and contrast for living conditions and risks around the world. Without it as a reference, as a presence that we keep at bay in our periphery, how can one appreciate life for what it is?

If we would only be so invested in our bodies that we could see the progression of unhealthy habits and risk factors giving rise to diseases. And, in fact, even now, we are beginning to do that. Possibly, when more engaged, we would conscientiously choose to prolong life instead of simply toying with delaying death.

A book on dying and death must maintain a focus on the living if a person's final acts are to be results of choice. Keeping an eye as best one can on health and wellness, risk factors, and signs and symptoms of progression and development of diseases and their building blocks is essential if detection, control, reversal, and eradication are desired. These risk factors may serve as forewarnings that death can and will close in if not controlled and repelled. Death must not catch one sleeping, for when it comes, as if a thief in the night, it is often a preventable robbery. We must maintain the active drive to live as long as we can but understand that the time will come when death calls, and our answer will change to an acceptance of goodbye.

Life and health

Living and dying are intertwined, interconnected. In life, we age in phases: one in ascending steps of improvement and growth, the second in decremental decline. The first begins at birth and ascends; the second in later youth and descends. The two curves cross in midlife. So loss of brain and kidney cells, a slow process, decreases the capacities of these systems over time. This death of cells, which is also represented in other systems, marks the beginnings of the end of life, our deaths.

Life takes us through seasons of environmental change. With changes, we are exposed to new experiences, and time passes; we age and pass through stages of life. The process is a journey. In living our lives, we progress and grow. Our environment continually changes, and we adapt, changing in our bodies and minds in order to cope. We adjust—preparing for what lies ahead. The environment, genetic predispositions, and parental nurturing and nudging provide the matrix for our behavior. Through our experiences, we adjust, and life molds us toward maturity. Managing the journey presents a struggle. We progress from innocence and naivety to maturity; through youth, middle, and older ages; from being healthy to developing diseases; through many different relationships, even marriage, on our trek to adulthood.

Presently, we are alive and, hopefully, healthy. The time for us to address longevity and dying is, perhaps, ideally now, while we have all our faculties. The time to realize that a foundation laid early to extend our lives and prepare us for a future, with as much happiness as life can bring, is now.

The young years

When young, we view ourselves as strong. We live moment to moment, sometimes with a plan and often out of impulse. We have unfounded hope, we deny reality, we do not worry about the future years, and we see ourselves as invincible. We only view our frailties and potential failures as belonging to someone else; it will not happen to us. The reality of life is that it can happen to each of us; it will happen and seems to come out of the blue.

It's easier to view such challenges in others, especially in the young, who continue to learn lessons from their experiences. Though we all dream that life will go well, we expect to work hard and expect obstacles. We all grumble, then force ourselves to work through them and move on.

Life is not to be wasted and is to be lived to the fullest with whatever one has been given. Though the life we have been given is influenced by society and culture, we are best taught to plan, and, if possible, whatever our state, prepare ourselves.

Life keeps giving lessons

Learning never stops. Life teaches us; other people teach us.

All we need to do is pay attention, listen, ask questions, read, do our homework, and keep learning. Ultimately, we are products of lessons learned and experiences we've struggled through.

The middle, transition years—both exciting and dull

Those middle years, the transition from youth to young adulthood and into the older years, move in a time frame that depends on one's view. An individual's life view originates with memories that forge our thinking and affect our choices. Even during struggles, it's how one perceives the challenges that matters most, for seemingly rough waters filled with dangerous events may be remembered as smooth sailing when one looks back. It was an adventure, and though problems arose, was still exhilaratingly fun.

Those transition years are invaluable for living. They are, indeed, meaningful years when family is forged and traditions are established for the young to carry on, struggles are faced and lived through, dreams developed—the essence of living, the backbone for the full life. Did we live or just survive?

Working years spent supporting families in a head-down, career-focused position often pass too fast, lacking fun. That's unfortunate, for life's to be fully appreciated even as we continue in the struggle. Focusing on the jobs of family and work may cause one to be too detailed and serious, taking attention away from the individuals with whom he or she lives and is trying to influence and guide.

Adjusting your focus to quality of life makes living the full life possible. This focus on the bigger picture and on family as a goal in and of itself increases possibilities for quality living. Such a life is attainable if cultivated. The quality of your life is to be actively pursued. If you do not, too much time slips away, the type of time that makes you wonder where you were and what you did—time without purpose. Though work and career are important, you may eventually realize they are only a means to an end. You may be remembered for the work, but odds are, who you are in your family will give more opportunities for fulfillment in life. It will come through your efforts to help your spouse and children reach their highest potential in their lives.

There is a balance between family and work. Each person sets this for himself or herself and in so doing finds purpose. Our greatest gift to ourselves and others is to recognize and nurture the service we give, both at home to our families and at work. Acts of serving foster meaningful relationships, and, as we serve, we think and behave differently. In performing as a spouse, parent, or worker, we have more purpose for each of the things we do. Since we are then responsible to the service, it's easier to avoid taking things personally and to interact, function, and perform better.

How will I be remembered?

Though humans are strong and tough, we are at the same time delicate and frail.
    Do we appreciate what we have?
    Do we appreciate those with whom we live?
    Do we express our love?
    Do we show we care?
    What are the values of the "full life"?
    How will we—I—be remembered?

Benefits of healthy living choices

Experts recommend that you seek supportive friendships and follow a regular routine of physical exercise, including a majority of aerobic activities such as daily walking, with isometric exercise using mild weights, all for toning muscles and maintaining fitness. And eat a healthy diet. This is all good common sense.

Since we have an interest in the whole span of life, let us better view longevity from the far side, from the older side. Centenarians have been targeted in numerous spots around the world, not scattered here and yon. What has extended their lives? Did they develop common, healthy interests that emphasized simple recommendations for a full life legions ago? Did they predict they would live longer if they collectively followed a certain plan? No, of course not, for they were not organized for that purpose, and life could not give them that guarantee. Maybe it began as a tribal tradition.

Through studies of these groups, there are common habits that we can list. There is, of course, extensive research to assist you in developing your own individual program, but here is an account of what they do as general recommendations for each of us. It is purposely kept short and simple. It is certainly a wealth of knowledge, a healthy place to begin as we work toward the goal of longer, healthier, and happier living.

Centenarian's pattern of habits for health and happiness

- Stay active. Maintain brisk walking and other exercises regularly.
- Divert stress. Rest adequately, laugh, don't worry, and surrender, for you are not in control anyway.
- Eat enough. Eating less than a full meal is adequate—that's about 80 percent.
- Eat less meat. Focus on plant-based diets heavy on vegetables and fruits, with only moderate intake of fish. Limit meat, poultry, refined grains and sugar; include nuts, olive oil, beans (fava, black, and soybeans), and lentils. Avoid processed foods, pasta, and white starches.

- Drink wine with meals: two glasses for men and one for women (wine has properties that reduce heart disease, cancer, and the progression of neurological disorders such as Alzheimer's and Parkinson's diseases).
- Be social. Attend regular social events; community is healthy.
- Maintain your faith. Attend services regularly and ensure you feel you are included.
- Keep family first and foremost. Listen and stay meaningfully involved.

The full life

So for each individual, the quest for and the ability to make change happen creates freedom to pursue the full life. A life less bound by worries from the past or about the future, or less weighted with imagined fears and anxiety, is within everyone's reach. Understanding what it is creates the desire for it, although it will not displace focus, determination, and hard work. That comes from excitement and self-encouragement about the project, of what to do and enthusiasm that "I can do this." Part of the full life involves utilizing one's whole being—making use of all one's assets that result from interacting with others; from the accumulation of our knowledge and experience with various skill sets and education and how we adapt in applying what we do know; from our ability to visualize components and unite them into functional units and create a business or make a process function more efficiently. Essentially, our skill sets make use of all our assets that, when combined with a keen awareness to circumstances, create opportunity to make things happen.

We only need to free ourselves from all the roadblocks that interfere with the process of moving forward, from those disadvantages that originated from our backgrounds—the way we were treated by others who forged our attitudes and belief systems and created our negative self-talk. We can release the outworn, repetitive, and discouraging messages within our heads and delete them. Real freedom removes these shackles and enables us to move, to take charge of ourselves, to accept challenges, to take risks, and to grow.

From the Christian religion, Jesus said, "I have come that they may have life, and have it to the full" (John 10:10, NIV). Jesus's involvement in one's life implies specific matters of faith and belief. The quote is not interpreted to forecast prosperity, but rather hope for freedom from burdens and the opportunity for change, confidence, and the ability to do. Both Western religion and Eastern philosophy promote a life without worry about the past or future; foster the acceptance of self, others, and current life circumstances; and encourage kindness and forgiveness and reaching out to others for the good of all. All are essential. The components foster motivation, accountability, responsibility, reliability, transparency, and encouragement; all lead to producing an independently dependent individual—the goal.

More years and more changes

Over the years, there are so many memories, so many stories to tell. The years fly by. The children grow up and venture out on their own. Now my loved one and I are alone together again. It is not to say it is the same as it was before children, for it is not. It is even better than that. When young, we shared the excitement of a life ahead, whereas now, there's a sense of calmness. There is work, but it is now more of a means to an end. We are not building lives with ambitious zeal. We are more content to live for today, to maintain and think of health and actively support it. We live to support each other. We live to be active and thankful and to have fun.

Life has its "oh, what's next" moments, but they are balanced with those fun moments. Fun may be a matter of definition. It is a good feeling, to be savored while it lasts. One has to be vigilant to both see and feel it. It's a sharable moment. Life and struggles promote a seriousness that can override fun, but it must be overcome and fun regained. Fun is light. Fun is laughter. Fun is there between the frequent, small problems that recur daily. Life is not always about disasters—sick family members, trouble with the car not working, pipes bursting in the cold or worse. But since they may happen, it is best to make the most of them and enjoy the times in between. Taking time to plan for hard times, both in the home and on the road, with options for solutions, helps diminish the stress later when problems do strike.

Life continues in the struggle

We need plans for our education, our careers, and our health. There is purpose to all we do and consequences to each decision and choice we make.

Our anticipation of retirement parallels vacation as a time for fun, enjoyment, and immunity from life's problems. Life's struggles happen to older people after all their life experiences and even after retirement. They have problems with medical issues, where to live, affording this and that, how to fill out various forms as part of daily business that continues to go on, and more. Challenges continue to come at us all; there's no group that's immune. It is, however, the time to use all those experiences and accumulated knowledge to solve whatever problems life presents.

The challenges can accumulate to the point that people will reconsider their beliefs and what they stand for. That's normal thinking.

The stresses associated with the death of someone who has been a part of us, whom we have depended on and loved, with whom we have spent lots of time and experienced life is overbearing and heartbreaking. We know that death happens to others but overlook the impact it has on the families and friends of those left behind. For those experiencing the loss, it is as though the world has stopped. When it happened to me, I wondered if anybody noticed. Couldn't they see my hurts and pains as if they were visible? No, it did not appear to affect them at all. The losses—some of our own and always of others—have different degrees of significance in their effects upon us. Some bother us, and some do not. It is respectful to acknowledge and empathize with any loss felt by others.

Life is stressful in the older years

Throughout my career, the older folks have made note of the stresses in their lives. Older age, even with a wealth of experiences, does not make life's difficulties and challenges any easier. And as frail as some older people appear, they endure more illnesses, trauma, strife, and stressors in general than I thought they could.

It has been my privilege to attend to the health of others in their later years who have thrived on sports accomplishments, even going to the trouble of training for, entering, and winning medals in the Senior Olympics for their age groups. Their physical-fitness battles help them feel better, endure stress and illness more easily, and recover more quickly when ill or injured. They stay active, get out and about more, have more interests, take better care of themselves, and are less depressed. They eat and sleep better. They are self-selected survivors whom studies predict will do well.

Examples of older, ordinary folks

Olga's a ninety-four-year old competitive champion and an inspiration! She keeps healthy by staying on her feet and maintaining an active schedule. Her weekly calendar is filled with physical activities, and those activities are undergirded by special people who provide her with friendship and support. Attending to these activities keeps her busy. She's revved up her aspirations for achievements since retiring from teaching school—in track and field, of all things! Her reward is lots of medals and feeling great and healthy. She was featured in a *Parade* magazine article by Bruce Grierson (he authored the book *What Makes*

Olga Run?, released in January 2014) to show the benefit of exercise in keeping her youthful and healthy. PhD geneticist Angela Brooks-Wilson was quoted as saying that longevity is thought to be 70–75 percent related to lifestyle. So it seems to be a matter of choice.

The article highlighted the support staff surrounding Olga, but it did not suggest that the support and the reinforcing medals won from the competition were instrumental in giving her renewed life and good health. She and her staff share common interests. Their friendship and camaraderie are likely sealed by the relationships, the glue that keeps each of them coming back for more. Of course, there are many benefits from exercise, as there are from eating properly, but you can bet that these attachments either reinforce those from very early in life or give her an opportunity to refresh and rebuild what was lacking back then.

Jim has been advised to cut back on heavy physical activities now that he's "older." He finds it is hard to do. He has had a real struggle; change is hard. It is difficult to ask a younger, slower-moving guy to take over. It's asking for help, something he does not do. To ask feels like giving up, particularly to someone he thinks will be careless or do an inadequate job, someone he sees as still learning his or her own job.

It should be seen as a giving in, not a giving up. It takes courage. It is a type of pacing oneself, conserving energy, and avoiding the risk of injury. It is letting go. It is giving the job to someone who can do X in his own way as you did it your way. Better? Probably not. Focus on the job alone, and it will be easier to give in.

Jody had coronary artery bypass surgery ten years ago and was doing well from that standpoint. He was able to stay physically active, even though other problems made him quite frail. He could not sit still, so he continued to struggle with household things men do, but he persisted until finishing the task. Overly fatigued and near completion of a recent project, he slipped, fell, and broke his ankle. The question is, just what effect will that fracture have on his future and on his health, both cardiac and noncardiac? Will he be able to rehabilitate himself and return to his usual routine, or will it be a life-changing event? It seems we have to stay in shape and be "street-smart." When young, we denied the future ills, and it was healthy; now, we cannot deny even the chance of falling. We need to embrace and fear it. Falling can seal our fate and is to be respected and avoided, even at the cost of slowing down. In our routines, we move, turn, and walk briskly as ever, but now we had best change to be safer or risk a bad break that would rob our independence. We have to change.

John is in his nineties and is as active as he was at seventy, with energy that impresses. He underwent anesthesia for colon cancer. He had colon surgery for a cancerous polyp years ago. He would forget things occasionally but otherwise had no medical issues but age. After a thorough preoperative evaluation, it was decided there was no contraindication to proceed with surgery again. This time, he suffered delirium postanesthesia.

One month into recovery, he worsened. Not only mentally, but physically. He had trouble walking and teetered; he repeated himself and was occasionally confused. It was as if his motivation and energy had abandoned him and he had aged beyond his years. Thankfully, he hadn't injured himself falling.

He made the rounds with his physicians and specialists too. A young neurologist claimed he was "old" and this is what happens in life. This, of course, enraged John and his family to no end. Consulting another neurologist tempered the reality of the change. All felt better, though they knew the improved demeanor would not change the problem or potential outcome. Physical therapy and volunteering to take time off from work did not help. The more the problems persisted, the older and more discouraged John felt.

Is it more about the doctor's presentation—and manners—that makes such a difference in a patient's reception and perception?

We each desire and prefer to be treated with respect and dignity, to be given a little "sugar," so to speak, with the awful-tasting medicine—a more gentle choice of wording but still a truthful assessment.

Taking care

"Old" is undeniable, but it's not necessarily the label or destination of choice. Although we are closer to the end than at any time in our lives, the label does not have the power to predict our outcome. Some of us unique individuals may be more youthful and more active than many others even younger than we are. As we age, either with glee, or kicking and screaming and taking on the challenges of the relentless number of problems that develop, being labeled "old" is forced, from someone too removed from us and our plight to appreciate it. Though we do not like it, we realize others, especially those younger, will still use the "old" label, and we will adjust. "Older" is better for me. It's easier to chew and swallow, accept and process.

Fond memories—from people and experiences

During our older years, most of us have family and friends who are even older. The pace of their lives varies. Some people decline more rapidly than others, and some seem to stay youthful forever. Life is a hill to climb, but the thrill is more on the upside. Often in life, emptiness and depression come after the challenge of the climb is done. Cockiness and self-adulation also result, but neither sustains us, for there is always the next mountain to climb. Unlike on the ski slopes, the thrill is on the downside—speeding and coasting in the free fall. On the upside, while riding up to the mountaintop, we daydream, enjoy the view, and anticipate the run.

How do we remember the experiences? It depends on how we spent the time. Time seems to pass quickly when we are involved and focused on the task or when having fun. Memories also depend on the people we were with. What is it that maintains your passion? Was the thrill all about the work? Do we remember the people with whom we were involved? Did we include our loved ones, or were family issues separate and out of bounds? Do we realize how long it's been? How much time did pass? How old are we now? What was all that effort worth? What do we really have to show for the time and energy expended? Was it a good and meaningful life? Were there any lessons learned?

Well, the life spent during those days and events is past. Who remembers the absences felt, where the time went, or who benefited? It's gone.

The thing to do is to live hard and get the most out of each day, as much as you want. There is only one life, and it is here in front of each of us. Though we get many chances to redo things and make up for losses, there is no gain in staying in the past except in an historical sense. And, while there, we actually progress backward. The present is the view for focus and the place to be to learn to live, for here is what life's current lessons are about: living in the moment. Life still presents challenges that, for older folks, bring new and different lessons to be learned. We receive no credit for previous experiences. We are only able to utilize those experiences and lessons learned as we work through the next set of problems, whatever they may be. We keep adjusting, for we are tough and have shown so before.

We forgot we have forgotten before

As we age, we forget things for a moment here and there. Mostly, we do not think about it. This tendency to forget begins earlier than most of us are aware of or admit to. As time goes on, we eventually refer to an awkward moment of forgetfulness; others recognize it as a "senior moment." It is something best taken in stride without angst or other reaction. It is best left unnoticed. It is a more worrisome phenomenon when it interferes with our interactions with others and especially if we are unaware of it. Recall seems to worsen if we let it frustrate us; it is best to stay calm and not interrupt conversations.

Continue in the struggle—we have overcome before

Age is no reason to back off. Life may not be fair, but we must continue trudging up the next hill. Realizing that life's struggles do not lighten up, that we still have new lessons to learn, and that we can learn to control the downhill run are assignments for us as part of the older set. We may not continue at paying jobs in our chosen vocations, but we can still use the tools we have learned to carry on—tools learned at work, in class, online, or at a conference, or ones we picked up here and there. These tools, or lessons learned, are the backbone of our skills to solve problems in our daily lives. You, as an experienced and knowledgeable individual, can even consider volunteering to teach the next generation in your profession.

Life continuously presents us with struggles and challenges with our own health and that of family members, with family problems that come and go, with maintenance of the house, with decisions regarding transportation or the question of when to stop driving, and with the handling of financial issues. Certainly, by now, we know when we need help from others or from professionals and know how to obtain what we need. Our struggles, however, are about the business of living and are things we need to deal with, to solve and resolve. Overall, the important people—our families and our friends—furnish the quality, the essence of the full life. In this process, we have learned the importance of enjoyment, of having more fun and doing everything possible to live as long as we can.

9
Disease

Our approach to living reflects the way we die

It is our individual duty to stay healthy. We need to be aware of our family's health and follow a healthy lifestyle. Yes, our ancestors ate heartily, but they were more active as they toiled the land. If we are not so active, we need to attend to health risks as though our lives depended on them, for they do.

Disease development is the fate of man. We are all vulnerable. For some diseases, we know the causes and risk factors. There are many that give no warning. They may be influenced by genetics, but often more by environmental issues related to what we do as hosts.

Diseases affect us all. With some, we are victims, and with others, we increase the risk through our choices. Anyone who smokes; drinks heavily; is inactive; is overweight; has hypertension, high cholesterol, or diabetes mellitus; lives or works in a polluted environment; uses illicit drugs; and/or lives on the street is at risk. Food choices, such as salt, sugar, and fat (lard), aggravate specific diseases, and the processing of foods increases our risks all the more. We could certainly avoid these and develop new tastes. Though our mothers taught us what tastes "good," there is more to food than taste alone.

Many folks now have had joint replacements. Often the rehab efforts are painful and rugged. The lesson is to simply stay physically active, lest one joint at a time degenerates from wear and tear with signs and symptoms of stiffness, joint pains and physical deconditioning to follow. Weakness, falls, injuries, wrong decisions, and missed or excess medications may occur and enter the circle at any point to aggravate any worsening conditions, contributing to a negative vicious cycle. While one battles other problems, even cognitive dysfunction may become manifest or, if in subclinical form, significantly worsen. Research data predicts our health shifts in proportion to our activity level, so our task is to push ourselves, as best we can, to exercise regularly.

Common diseases, often present in "clusters"

Let's list some specific diseases that affect us older folks.

>   Coronary artery disease and myocardial infarction
>   Hypertension
>   Atrial fibrillation
>   Strokes
>   Diabetes mellitus
>   Peripheral vascular disease
>   Chronic kidney disease
>   COPD (chronic obstructive pulmonary disease)
>   Cancer
>   Dementia
>   Degenerative joint disease
>   Obesity
>   Infectious diseases
>   Cognitive dysfunction

There are many combinations of diseases that affect us. This disease list does not include accidental—unintentional—injuries that occur commonly. Any one of these problems alone presents challenges, but in combinations, they make life especially difficult. For example, congestive heart failure is often associated with other comorbidities, meaning it clusters with hypertension, diabetes mellitus, obesity, coronary artery disease, chronic kidney disease, and anemia. And certainly, accidents present added stresses by often uncovering frail organ systems, which adds to complications.

The combinations of these medical problems compound the many burdens for the patient and further expand the care needed. Of course, the intent is for earliest discovery with the goal of control and, if possible, reversal of the disease. Early treatment can put a given disease—for instance, early onset type-two diabetes mellitus—on temporary hold and add time before full manifestation. It requires attention to detail, namely regular exercise and better food choices. But with further delay, it is unfortunate that the detrimental processes may advance significantly by the time of discovery. That means the process is ahead of us, but it does not mean we cannot "catch up" to a point of stability. Then, there is disappointment when one finds one's disease to be far advanced, beyond the point of return, calling for salvage and survival tactics at the time of diagnosis. In each case, it takes a community of effort for success. First, the patient's commitment, and often the family's, is essential. In spite of these possible scenarios, the initial focus remains on discovery, prevention, and control, and then, eventually, stopping the causes and eradicating the disease.

The medical profession is to be ultrasensitive in caring for people, whatever their state of health, whether focusing on wellness and prevention, managing multiple risk factors that are precursors for more serious illnesses that usually develop into clusters of diseases, caring for sick patients in the outpatient or inpatient settings, or helping those who have chosen alternative paths or decided on no treatments at all. We are mandated to achieve improvements using evidence-based treatments.

Even though providers are mandated to successfully manage patients' health care, patients find reasons for noncompliance—not following guidelines given for possibly reversing diseases and/or achieving better health. It often seems that we patients do not understand the significance of disease and how far along the disease has progressed before discovery. It is not envisioning it worse than it is, but time is of the essence. Best we pay attention, notice change, check it out with action, and see our physician. And we, as patients, may have the same diseases as many others in our families, but it is to our advantage to avoid adopting family members' outdated attitudes; to be in charge of ourselves; and to manage what we eat, stay active, understand the purpose of taking the meds, and comply with the treatment plan. We need to do everything possible to change our habits. It's best to take personal ownership, learn to manage our disease(s), and protect our future.

Compliance with disease management

Data indicates that overall, we patients do not take care of ourselves, in that only 20 percent take the recommended medications and comply with their doctors' recommendations. It seems that hypertension heads the list of diseases that are undertreated. Though stroke and heart attack rates have diminished over the last half century due to the benefits of modern medicine, other problems have escalated to stir the mix in the wrong direction, such as obesity and diabetes mellitus and over the last twenty years heart failure and atrial fibrillation have been observed more frequently. Though tracking charts show benefits and reduced costs in many areas of medicine over these years, the improvements stand out in contrast to the additional costs and unique challenges for treatment and control accompanying these rising diseases.

It is clear that there are consequences and costs to each decision and change in life, including guidelines for care. Though we are making progress, the processes used may not always be guiding patients down paths that are in their best and future interests, as exemplified by past recommendations that replaced cholesterol in diets with higher carbohydrates and processed sugars and the resulting consequences: accentuating some of the diseases noted above. The goal is always to change patients' health behaviors based on solid scientific evidence, then, translating the data through educational and experiential processes, giving the evidence to professionals who in turn, evaluate, diagnose and treat the population. A goal is for diagnosis early enough in a patient's exposure to their diseases, that they may become engaged and better understand the need for change and willingly take ownership of the process and, thus, improve compliance.

Hazards to obesity: clustering, loss of mobility, and death

Common sense says that health risks worsen as we become older and heavier. A recent study published in *JAMA Internal Medicine* followed older women as they aged from their early seventies to the mideighties and found just that. "As the women aged toward eighty-five years, the authors found five distinct groups. Nearly 20 percent were healthy, meaning they added no major chronic diseases and maintained their original weight and their mobility. Nearly 15 percent began the study with one or more of five chronic diseases (cancer, heart disease, stroke, diabetes, or hip fracture), didn't add any new ones, and maintained their original weight and mobility. Nearly one-quarter developed one or more diseases during the study time and maintained their ability to walk. Another 18 percent did lose mobility or reported limited ability to walk a block or climb a flight of stairs. They essentially lost their independence. The remaining women, nearly a quarter of them, died before age eighty-five. Thus, 43 percent deteriorated as a result of the combined disadvantages of progressive, obesity-aggravated loss of mobility, and the propensity to add on diseases."

The double loss of mobility and independence added to the disease burdens to significantly impact health and function. Dr. Rillamas-Sun said, "We found that women with a healthy body weight had a greater chance of living to 85 without developing a chronic disease or a mobility disability. The heavier you are, the worse your chances of healthy survival." The article further noted, "Compared to older women with healthy body mass indexes (below a B.M.I. of 25), overweight women had a 20% greater chance of developing one of the five diseases. Women with obesity (B.M.I. over 30, but below 35) had a 65% higher risk of disease, and women with higher levels of obesity were more than twice as likely to develop disease. The likelihood of dying before age 85 showed a similar pattern."

This is costly to the individual and family in many ways. We know it will be a huge price to pay, and the bill is on the way. We will each pay in different ways. This is a problem that has to be viewed and addressed from the fifty-thousand-foot altitude level. Reversing the trend of weight increases in both children and adults is society's task. Deciding the strategy is the challenge. Where does it begin? Does it begin in the legislature, the corporate boardroom, or in the home? This is beyond our scope. For us, the focus has to be on the ground level: with the individual and family in community.

Our goal is to encourage increased activity and portion control at mealtime. Overweight, older folks may best be served by visiting a physical therapist before muscle weakness sets in and affects not only strength but balance, with an increased risk of falling. Daily I hear, "I can't get out because…," "I don't feel like doing…," "This or that bothers me…," "My pain affects my…," and "No, I don't want to take simple pain pills; I already take too many meds." These comments come from the other side of "I must keep going." If such negative self-talk messages are not overcome, one will lose ground.

These messages begin as complaints about needing to exert effort to maintain activity, but they can quickly degenerate into "I can't" and then "I'm too tired and don't want to anymore."

These messages predict further worsening in both attitude and structural elements, which may begin the downward spiral unless supportive efforts are successful in turning around such behaviors. Hypervigilance is key to detecting and counteracting these negative forces to which we each may be exposed.

All bodily systems interconnect

Risk factors for many diseases stir the immune system to promote an inflammatory response. Because of the persistent presence of the risk factors, inflammation continues. Inflammation that does not turn off creates disrepair and disease. By design, all systems are connected; here, the immune system overlaps with the cardiovascular system, for they share common risk factors that are associated with diseases. The agitated immune system spreads and in this case affects both immunity and defensive systems. Thus, coronary heart disease and cancer have ties that bind. Though we feel victorious in assisting people through the many problems associated with their cardiovascular disease, they often develop and succumb to the rigors of cancers, especially lung and colon cancer. Therefore, vigilance for change in signs and symptoms is indicated. As the diseases, including leukemia, develop, they rob one's energy and cause one to feel worse, to develop other symptoms, or to show signs of hemorrhage and bruising. On recognition, the patient must be reevaluated by his or her physician. Sometimes, in these cases, we need to repeat tests, even though they were checked and found normal a few months before, for changes happen. Rechecking the basic blood counts six months later in one patient who voiced persistent changes led to the diagnosis of acute leukemia.

Maximize better health measures and rehab when needed

Tammy was a ninety-year-old lady in a nursing home after suffering a broken hip. Her kidneys were failing, and her mild cognitive dysfunction worsened. It was clear she could no longer live alone. She resisted any help that came in and, at times, even physically attacked the staff attending to her. After a few years in a nursing home, she said she was "hanging on with no purpose" and was miserable. She no longer enjoyed life. She had suffered through a number of chronic illnesses that had challenged her since youth, including hepatitis, hypertension, and a large stroke from which she had recovered. Suffering had never dampened her spirit for living life to the fullest. She often had cut short rehab or follow-up recommendations, for the efforts needed for completion seemed excessive and she felt that continuing them was unnecessary. Though she had always been frail and accustomed to not feeling well, these latest struggles were overwhelming. Like other devoted mothers, she lived thinking her purpose was to always be there for her children, who themselves were now older adults and quite capable of caring for themselves. On one of her more lucid days, she called them in and informed them of her plan to die. She wanted reassurance that they would be OK without her. When they confirmed they would be OK, she acted. She had been contemplating her end for a while and intended to stop eating and to stop all her medications; she had lost her will to live. She died within the week. Though they were saddened and grieved their loss, to this day, they are convinced their mom was at peace and life's end had been kind to her.

Mimicking family members may be problematic

Many of us grew up with parents and grandparents who had negative feelings and experiences associated with many aspects of health care. We must recognize that life was harder then. Because of strong family ties in those times, we learned those attitudes from them and had them reinforced by others and even through our own experiences. We think we are following our own free wills, but are we? Our guidance first came from others, and we may be following their desires when we think they are ours. We truly need to make our attitudes and actions our own and shed the outworn ones we have learned. That is one of the first steps we might take to be our own health advocates, finally be our own bosses, make our own decisions, and exercise our own free will.

Of course, with certain diseases and medications, we do not feel good and motivated to do our "homework" and take good care of ourselves. In this state, and with previously learned attitudes, how do we change the focus for our own benefit? If you are revisiting your doctor, it will be a wise investment to have this conversation, for it may change your life. The doctor will provide some time to talk, because he or she knows just how powerful an issue it is and how much his or her help will benefit you. Tell the doctor about your state of affordability for tests, treatments, and follow-up and about the support or lack of it at home. These problems may be the reasons you are not eating healthily, taking your medications correctly, or sleeping well. Each of these items contributes to your ability to work on yourself and will be worth your time. These issues rob you of energy, increase the angst within you, raise your blood pressure risks, and sap you of your health. They interfere with living the full life and enjoying your family and loved ones. In this state, you are not the free person you may see yourself to be.

If you are young or middle-aged, health issues can be tough enough. If you are well and never give your future any thought, now is the time to plan for your future. Doing a little homework will go a long way. Talking with your doctor will go a long way. Saving a little money now, when younger, in a retirement fund will go a long way. These things are all about you and are equally important. Seek out good and trusted resources to assist you with these tasks—the earlier the better.

Be vigilant

For the older set, when do you realize that, though you still have the perception you are as active, eating as much, and as healthy as when you were younger, you are actually not? We are not talking about being more forgetful, for we all own a piece of that.

Be observant of yourself and take note. It may even be helpful to write down experiences annually and review your thoughts and feelings over the years. It helps in planning for your future. These changes may begin when your spouse or partner is distracted, working, or depressed and can't help, or is taking care of other family members—a time when your usual routine is off balance. The same can be said if you sprain an ankle or your back. You're off balance. During those times, you don't eat as well, and you are less active, sleep less, stay inside more, and experience many little things that overload you. You then feel bad and are less motivated to live the more healthy life. You are then deep in the trenches of life and cannot see your plight. We have all experienced some of this, and if persistent, can lead to more chronic misery. If these conditions persist, you are in trouble.

Members of the older set may begin to slip, and neither they nor we recognize the change. It may occur when they persistently feel bad after an injury or illness. This may result in a reduction in their circles of activities and, simultaneously, if they do not eat sufficiently, their stomachs may shrink, making eating uncomfortable. After a while, weight loss, lack of conditioning, social isolation, and loneliness ensue. They do not want to be bothered, and, at the same time, they do not want to trouble others. If it happens to us, we might miss some of our medications and deteriorate further. We do not realize that we have stopped rowing our boats and are being swept back by life's negative currents, thereby losing ground. This is stressful. No wonder we become discouraged and are unable to see the negative changes as they begin and are no longer able to take care of ourselves to correct it. We were blind to things brewing, whether with or without symptoms. If someone else voices concern before we worsen, we will deny symptoms and signs of illness and blame them on something else or say we will wait a little longer and see if they disappear on their own.

Eventually, we are surprised when something bad happens. We can feel just as bad if some of the same things are going on beneath the surface while we are lost in our work or out pursuing a surrogate pleasure.

During these times, we need more help than we realize. It is a time to listen to feedback from friends and family. They can help us recognize these things that affect us, our health, and our lives. Of course, now, when we don't need the extra help, is the time to have talks with those around us who are willing to assist. So please begin those conversations now.

Added Care

Our future may include discussing a change to provide us more help. The options may include more assistance in the home, moving in with children, moving to an assisted living facility, or moving into a nursing home.

These will be the times you might expect more forceful instructions from family members, reflecting a tone none other than your own. It would be beneficial if you could coach them before the need arises, to devise a script acceptable for both you and them. We all need help communicating meaningfully in these difficult times of change. Each of us will have a turn, and how we handle it reflects who we are, how stubborn we are, the state of our cognitive function, our history, and how we have lived. Be the person you are deep inside. Remove the protective shells and live life to the fullest, taking advantage of all your support and resources available. Those resources are right there in front of you. Open your eyes and talk.

Cognitive dysfunction stands out

I have followed numerous patients who had progressive memory loss beginning in their late sixties and early seventies. I was concerned they had the beginnings of dementia, and they may have, but the confusion, getting lost, and significant cognitive dysfunction was not apparent until into their nineties. It seemed that the symptoms were aggravated by illnesses such as pneumonia, atrial fibrillation, or fears struggling with cancer.

It's unfortunate to develop diseases. Each of us might best consider cause and effect and change whatever it takes to avoid diseases. For those who develop cognitive dysfunction, there's little chance for considerations. In later stages of dementia and Alzheimer's disease, without memory and with lack of interactions between different brain areas vital for thinking through situations and communicating with others, there's no follow-through. It is as if the person just fades away. The essence of being human wanes as communication and reasoning progressively diminish or are lost.

Of course, as this change is progressing, people affected still express their rote opinions and can strongly argue about many things they want. They don't understand. They become frustrated and then express themselves with anger. Others are quiet and calm, easy to work with. The usual process of persuasion, continually trying to logically convince them, is no longer effective, and family members become frustrated and tend to argue back, recycling the behavior, especially as the patients repeat the same questions. We each feel the hurt for those with cognitive dysfunction and what we perceive they are going through. We have to realize that family members are sometimes the last to recognize the irrationality in thinking manifested in their loved ones. The patients persist in interacting as if they, the irrational ones, are able to reason, for they stubbornly stick to their points thinking they still have the ability and authority to control themselves and those with whom they are interacting. It is an awkward and sad situation. We eventually learn to avoid aggravating the situation by treating them with respect, understanding, and calmness. It does not help to feel anger toward them. It is best to treat them as people who are unable to reason and have difficulty hearing. And, even though they are able to react with familiar responses and are occasionally lucid, they are unable to think things through or act appropriately, especially when upset. Patiently acknowledging the repetitive comments is the best response.

On two clinic days, I was looking for and found a number of patients who had varying degrees of cognitive dysfunction. They each were unique, and, though similar, their individual personalities clearly showed through the fog. The majority of them were aware of their memory loss, although a few did not recognize it and seemed genuinely surprised each time they were told their memory was "off." Most accepted cues from others to correct them. They argued through rationalization or denial or were outright blind to the lapse. Some simply laughed it off.

It appears that atrial fibrillation, hypertension, carotid artery disease, different varieties of heart failure, the presence of implanted pacemakers, chronic pain, depression, and inordinate stresses are outstanding problems those patients—ages sixty-six to ninety-one—collectively face day to day. Regrettably, dementia occurred in each of these people in spite of quick diagnosis and control of each of the diseases.

Most of these patients also had risk factors for vascular disease. Chronic pain and stresses would understandably aggravate many other issues, including hypertension, and place doubt on compliance with medications. One of the patients' husbands previously had recalcitrant hypertension and had had multiple strokes that resulted in severe dementia, necessitating confinement in a nursing home, where he later died.

So chronic disease limits the person, while each additional condition has a negative influence on other diseases that often occur in clusters. Thus, the patient suffers even more. Many diseases are associated with inflammation, which creates health burdens. The greater the burden or persistence of risk factors, the greater the inflammation, producing a vicious cycle. The greater the inflammation, the greater the body's defenses needed to rally. After a while, the defenses fatigue, and they may eventually fail. The success or failure depends on many things: the effects of the individual burden of the disease, the presence of other diseases, and the person's age. Each individual has diminishing reserves the older she or he becomes and the longer the diseases have been present. Thus, the patient's age and the duration of disease are variables that increase the burden on the body's repair and energy resources.

There are, of course, other diseases with overwhelming challenges. They, too, may be associated with pain and suffering, complications from chemotherapy, or hope-draining remissions/recurrences, especially metastatic cancer. Though the disease process can be similar when comparing two individuals, it is quite different, depending on circumstances. Cancers bring special fears absent in many other diseases. They affect elders as well as the young. Some younger people have their whole lives in front of them; others have begun families with small children. Some are in their waning, twilight years and suffer with other diseases with risks of complications and worsening status.

It's heartbreaking in every case, whatever the devastating disease, but it seems more threatening and serious in the young and in those with families to think of. They are all robbed of so much. The struggle to prolong life leaves them with pain and suffering that may interfere with their focus on family. They must develop supportive resources as they balance all their efforts with disease and family issues. They are forced to face their diseases, as well as the fears and anger known to exist, while striving to be an encouragement and an example for the family.

Family role model/leader maintained his hope for life until death

A young man once presented with a large myocardial infarction at an outlying hospital emergency department where I was moonlighting prior to entering private practice. After he was stabilized, we transported him to a larger hospital, where he recovered. He suffered damage in the attack and had loss of strength in his heart muscle to the point that he had heart failure requiring medications for further stability. He was unable to work. His risk of erratic heartbeat irregularities required a defibrillator. He was disabled for more than thirty years.

Follow-up labs documented an acute leukemia. Quick consultation with hematology/oncology predicted he had only two weeks to live without emergent treatment. He was admitted into the appropriate hospital and underwent chemotherapy treatments, and the leukemia went into remission. Over the next five years, he required three additional admissions for IV chemo treatments and responded favorably, and the leukemia went into remission. The last white count, however, did not respond as favorably as in the past.

He was a very kind and appreciative person the whole time I knew him. He once came to a support group to discuss end-of-life issues. He essentially taught the class how he fared all those years in his predicament: he was thankful he was able to play as much golf as he had and to enjoy his growing family over the years. He knew his life expectancy was short, and this less-than-full remission meant he likely would not respond as in the past. He was still thankful in spite of his condition and was at peace to the end; he died within a few months.

10
CONTINUING IN THE STRUGGLE

"LIVE LIFE TO THE FULLEST.
AND, IF HAPPINESS COMES YOUR WAY, SAVOR IT."
—*Anonymous*

Our capacity to move on is built in—from catastrophe to victory

People never stop amazing me. Though we have been discussing the more fearful and unknown side of these awfully serious issues, the person's world view is far different on reaching the other side. More than a few have gotten over acute illnesses that included signs of transient multiple organ failure and having doctors question their chances of survival. One man not only responded to treatment and continued recovery in rehab before going home, back in the office in follow-up he said with gusto, "Now I'm ready to get this knee replacement!" I am sure we do not forget that soon, but it is inherent within us that the drive for life goes on. There seems to be a quick recovery of the drive within us. Of course, when people encourage others with "Move on," it is understandably irritating and possibly inappropriate at the time. It is definitely better for the victim of all the problems to be the one to say it himself or herself, when he or she is ready.

We will all agree that those words have to come from within the affected person to be effective and to work positively.

Does aging and seeing friends die increase our awareness of the looming arm of death's reach?
    When we see people struggling, what are our thoughts?
    Do we contemplate their misfortunes as victims of disease processes?
    Do we wonder whether they have taken care of themselves as in living the full life?
    Does our increased awareness calm our anxiety that might cause us to flee? How can we know which way to run?
    Which direction is healthy?
    Do we support those struggling?
    Do we better attend to ourselves?
    Might our thought-through homework, if done in years past, kick in and lead us? Does our deeper thinking cause us to withdraw within or move outward and focus on the things we need to do with others?
    What do we want for ourselves?
    What is the full life?
    Are we living the full life?
    Do we desire to live the full life?
    What do we want for the rest of our time in this life?
    How do we prepare ourselves and others for our demise?

Being family—caring for one another through better parenting and grandparenting

How much do we care about our loved ones—our children and grandchildren?
    Does our love for them show through our actions?
    Now?
    In the past?
    Are we including them in our thoughts and plans for the future?
    What actions should we consider?

Have we taught them early on that we love them, shown them more than told them? Have we shared with them our positive visions for their futures because we caught a glimpse of their greatness through their actions?

Teaching involves showing, living with, involving, sharing, and experiencing, not just telling or instructing to read about life and skills.

Planning includes teaching and showing about relationships, family, studying, education, health, and careers.

Does our behavior with them reflect our visions and attitudes about them currently and for their future?

Can we envision them as successful when older?

Can we offer better parenting?

How soon are we a vision in our parents' eyes?

Where did the parents' hope begin? When they married? When we were developing within the womb? Yes, let's hope so.

Did they really think about us that soon?

Did they plan ahead?

For us?

If so, would our experiences in utero be different?

What is required in order for our parents or for us, as parents, to prepare and ensure a more favorable setting and outcome for the children?

What's the message for my own family, for my grandchildren?

To talk more and to share adults' life challenges. To no longer avoid mention of the struggles behind the scenes. It may be better for them, so they can learn something from adult experiences rather than be surrounded by a hedge of overprotection and silence. Of course, the conversation must be relevant to them so they'll receive it with meaningful influence. Otherwise, it is better left unsaid unless it's only intended to be another war story.

We will need to have planned, relaxing party times together to promote growth in our individual and collective relationships with both lighthearted and more meaningful conversations. At our family group meetings, everyone can have his or her say with appropriate give-and-take between family members who care about one another.

At the proper time and place in their lives, we need to assist our loved ones to make plans for everything, including retirement and end-of-life, before the need arises. Even at their ages, they need maps with compasses to point the way, elders as role models to observe, and discussions that keep everyone better prepared when the time arises.

Talking about these issues will improve living the struggle

We must begin to talk more about these subjects—dying and death. They are not taboo. We—I mean all of us and all willing and interested families—need to express educated opinions about each of these things. We have questions, and usually the answers are available because they are practical matters. Make plans to have those discussions. It needs to be done before ill health or cognitive dysfunction manifests and robs us older members from our families. We need to do this in hopes that we can recognize and arrange needed support. Perhaps we who are ill should have led these discussions years ago. But now we certainly need to express ourselves, our wishes, and our need for more help. Our families need to know we have hopes of improving or holding our own, that we will not necessarily die "before our time." We need them to be able to share their love and caring for us—we assume it is there, though it may be in hiding. We need to be more receptive, for we may have resisted their advice in the past and hampered their offers for assistance. They need to know that "I still want to be in charge, but I do want and need your help if you are willing and able to provide it." The process is worked out through discussions.

Tough transition: becoming your parent's parent

I know the transition is coming from my authority as my own boss and as the head of my family. I will eventually acquiesce and allow my caregivers, my hopefully loving family, to become my parents. One of the greatest privileges in life is for the child to become his or her parent's parent. We parents have hope that we will not require help, but we clearly want it when needed, though we resist. We try to hide that hope in the usual comments: "I don't want to put anybody to any trouble"; "I'll just stay home and not cause any trouble." Hope will be stifled until rekindled by a family member reaching out. Even if we are truly ready to die or death is inevitable, these encounters will still provide a closeness that only a caring person can give, and at the same time, give needed peace to the whole process. This will begin to happen through having focused and meaningful discussions about the issues, airing the wishes, and rehearsing the behaviors in preparation for a time when needed.

Of course, it is helpful for the givers and receivers to be cooperative and thankful for both the care and the privilege. Discussions may be prerequisites to voice these important details. If the discussions take place prior to the cognitive dysfunction, rehearsed and preferred statements may help both sides to reinforce more favorable responses, especially if presented in a more lighthearted manner. These rehearsed statements may provide a framework of behaviors on which to lean later when needed. These issues are ingredients to living life and approaching death, too, to the fullest.

Hope to find relief and renewal

Remember that having hope of a future makes it possible to receive and to reach out to others, to retake and reshape our lives going forward, to forecast how well we will do, and to summon our resources for action.

It is hope, faith, and love that keep the flame of life ignited. They are vital. We need each of them until the end. It's our hope, beliefs, and vision that can propel us into the full life.

Our hope, as we anticipate and approach death, is that we reconnect with our loved ones and that we experience no pain or distress and find peace.

Think it through. We humans seek connections. Attachments are very important to us. We were born attached by the umbilical cord and after delivery were closest to our moms and other surrogates, then to our fathers and siblings. All sorts of experiences began. Our automated, genetic smarts as a newborn took over. We saw, experienced, and learned who we were through the eyes of others. We had issues with feeding, toileting, and joining in with our new society. We coped and adapted. The attachments and connections were dependent on how we were treated and cared for.

There were opportunities for more coping and adapting as we grew. Each year brought challenges, and with those, the anatomy of our brains changed as we developed. Many parents assume the child can think in terms of action-consequences, but though they can mimic the more adult behaviors, judgments and the other skills are not fully developed until early adulthood. These are the times that the areas of emotion and executive functions are developed. Genes surely set up the matrix, but it seems it's not all genes and chemistry; environment has great influence. So both anatomy and function are essential.

If, through our upbringing or because of alterations in gene function, our ability to make attachments is altered from our familial norm, then we may withdraw or become more anxious during awkward or uncomfortable encounters with others. The resulting response is that we hesitate or refuse to connect with them. In those circumstances, we may seek connections and attachments with other things or people who may influence us in ways that may change our behaviors. The influence may in fact be negative or positive—not always predictably negative, though it would seem that way initially.

Humans seek relationships. We began that way, and if not satisfied and fulfilled, our internal drives, demanding satisfaction, seek surrogates. What satisfies us acts by stabilizing and comforting our brain's pleasure center.

Our experiences, including the attachments and connections we've had, contribute to making us who we are. Since we are now older, experienced, softened, and more open to others, we have the opportunity to recognize and release negative, binding, and restraining issues blocking us from connecting and continue changing for the better. That we can give and receive love is the essence of the good and full life. We need others. We need to connect. We need to assist those we care about in ways helpful to them and to improve communications. We can say we could have done more, but that's in the past. For now, it is best to let go the past and live for today. All we can do going forward is give, share, encourage, and influence by what we say and do—to connect. Our hope is in our connections.

Review of ingredients for healthy living

Perhaps we each should follow the centenarian's lifestyle – and add more items:
   Eat healthily.
   Avoid weight changes.
   Avoid processed foods.
   Avoid excesses in alcohol.
   Do not smoke.
   Seek out support.
   Be with others for companionship.

Be open to others' feedback.

Become vigilant for changes in your body and report them appropriately.

Push yourself to keep up mentally and physically.

Do not focus on your age.

Exercise daily; treat it like rehab and stretch—stay limber.

Slow down your pace; develop a healthy fear of falling.

Bring home your people skills used at work and make daily use of them.

Additional ingredients to consider for living the full life —

Don't worry.

Focus.

Live in the moment.

Be more accepting of you, others, your past, and current circumstances.

Be frugal.

Save for tomorrow.

Study and do your homework.

Plan – be prepared.

Talk.

Surround yourself with trusted friends and people smarter than you.

Collect more skills.

Reach out to others.

Let go of negative self-talk.

Delete all blame of self and others.

Have no guilt.

Control your emotions—let them motivate actions and solutions of issues.

Create positive self-talk and make your personal talents your new focus.

Learn to adjust and change.

Be balanced in life—take care of your family, health, social, and career projects.

In relationships—savor those special moments.

Connect with others.
Give, share, encourage, and influence.
Trust.
Live for today.
Live hard each day.
Enjoy family, friends, and memories.
Plan parties—get together with friends and family, have many hellos, and plan more goodbyes; celebrate life.
Have family meetings.
Listen more.
Be more selfless.
Be other oriented.
Make life easier—keep learning and use all your skills.
Be thankful and express it.
Self-reflect, change what needs to change, and express yourself.
Continue in the struggle.

Points to ponder

- Be heartened, for having an eye on dying positively impacts the quality of living.
- For the living, life becomes more challenging with age, and though they continue in the struggle, their view of death changes the closer it comes.
- Since we may die as we live, let's spend time to think it through and change.
- We are physical, intellectual, emotional, and spiritual, but the essence of living encompasses issues with meaning through relationships, love, enjoyment of the senses, spiritual growth, and the exercise of free will.
- To foster better relationships with our loved ones, we are to tell them we love, forgive, and thank them unendingly; we're to include them in our celebrations of life while we are living and teach them our approach to life, including our plans for dying.

- We always have opportunity for influence, especially in our families, so plan for it.
- Building legacy—how I will be remembered—is as important as preparing for career, family, and retirement.
- A special honor and privilege in life is the act of becoming a parent to parents.
- It is best to nurture your meaningful connections.

"Don't worry, be happy!" These words, meant to comfort, are taken from Bob Marley's song that suggests we look away from our sorrows, hurts, and depression; turn our focus away from our regrets; and not look ahead to the unknown, anxiety-producing future. Is this the definition of happiness? As the old song asks, "Is that all there is?" No. What's left is to serve others and enjoy and savor our relationships and opportunities as they come. To accept our present state and see and appreciate what is right in front of us—the day, our families, and problems. To deal with each of them; to work toward solving issues as they arise; to teach by sharing our stories from our experiences; to live within our means; to love and enjoy our families; and to help guide traditions and activities for great memories.

There are many gifts to be thankful for. They are to be utilized in life and in death. Savor the transition. Even now, there may be something about you that could conceivably influence someone else for a lifetime. Therefore, continue in the struggle, seeking and following the good and full life. Plan and prepare. Because by fostered your connections, you will leave footprints, memories, and influence behind as you head for the approaching joys and freedoms that extend your life into death—from here to eternity.

Appendix A

I. Advanced Directive or Living Will with or without Someone Assigned to Have Medical Power of Attorney

Organ donation

You can also specify in your advance directives any wishes you have about donating your organs, eyes, and tissues for transplantation or your body for scientific study. If you wish to donate your body for scientific study, contact the medical school closest to your home for details.

Share your wishes with your family

Injury, illness, and death aren't easy subjects to talk about, but by planning ahead, you can ensure that you receive the type of medical care you want. You also relieve your family of the burden of trying to guess what you'd want done. Be sure to discuss your wishes with your loved ones. Let them know you're creating advance directives and explain your feelings about medical care and what you'd want done in specific instances.

Fill out the forms for your state

Your advance directives should be in writing. Each state has its own laws regarding advance directives. Although it isn't required, you may want to consult an attorney about this process. State-specific forms are available from a variety of websites, such as the National Hospice and Palliative Care Organization.

Once you've filled out the forms, give copies to your doctor, the person you've chosen as your health-care agent, and your family members. Keep another copy in a safe but accessible place. You might also want to keep a card in your wallet that says you have a living will and where it can be found.

Review your advance directives from time to time

As your health changes or your perspective on life changes, you might reconsider some of your advance directives. Read them over from time to time to see if you want to revise any of the instructions. You can change your mind about your advance directives at any time.

To revise your advance directives, follow the same steps you used to create them. Get new advance directive forms to fill out. Discuss your changes with your friends, family, and doctor. Then distribute copies of the new advance directives and ask everyone to destroy the earlier version.

If there isn't time to redo the paper work, you can always cancel your advance directive by telling your doctor and your family. Remember, a living will or medical POA goes into effect only if you are unable to make medical decisions for yourself, as determined by your doctors.

II. Example of Living Will for the State of Georgia

LIVING WILL

      Living Will (declaration) made this ____ day of _____, 20__.

      I, _____, being of sound mind, willfully and voluntarily make known my desires that my dying shall not be artificially prolonged under the circumstances set forth below, do hereby declare:

If at any time I should have a terminal condition, become in a coma with no reasonable expectation of regaining consciousness, or become in a persistent vegetative state with no reasonable expectation of regaining significant cognitive function, as defined in and established in accordance with the procedures set forth in paragraphs (2), (9), and (13) of Code Section 31-32-2 of the Official Code of Georgia Annotated, I direct that life-prolonging procedures to my body (check the desired option)

____ including nourishment and hydration,
____ including nourishment but not hydration, or
____ excluding nourishment and hydration,
be withheld or withdrawn when the application of such procedures would serve only to prolong artificially the process of dying, and that I be permitted to die naturally with only the administration of medication or the performance of any medical procedure deemed necessary to provide me with comfort care or to alleviate pain.

In the absence of my ability to give directions regarding the use of such life-sustaining procedures, it is my intention that this declaration shall be honored by my family and physician(s) as the final expression of my legal right to refuse medical or surgical treatment and accept the consequences from such refusal.

I understand that I may revoke this living will at any time.

If I am a female and I have been diagnosed as pregnant, this living will shall have no force and effect unless the fetus is not viable and I indicate by initialing after this sentence that I want this living will to be carried out. _____ (initial)

I understand the full import of this declaration and I am emotionally and mentally competent to make this declaration.

Signed on this _____ day of _____, 20__, in the City of _____, County of _____, State of _____.

_____
(signature)

I hereby witness this living will and attest that: the declarant is personally known to me and voluntarily signed this writing in my presence. I believe the declarant to be at least 18 years of age. I am at least 18 years of age. I did not sign the declarant's signature above for or at the direction of the declarant. I am not related to the declarant by blood or marriage, and to the best of my knowledge am not entitled to any portion of the estate of the declarant according to the laws of intestate succession or under any will of declarant or codicil thereto, or directly financially responsible for declarant's medical care, and I have no present or inchoate claim against any portion of the estate of declarant. I am not the attending physician, and I am not an employee of a hospital, skilled nursing facility, or other health care facility in which the declarant is a patient.

First Witness:
_____, residing at
_____
(Signature Above)

Second Witness:
_____, residing at
_____
(Signature Above)

REFERENCES

Death

Aries, Philippe, *Western Attitudes toward Death*. Translated by Patricia M. Ranum. Baltimore: Johns Hopkins University Press, 1974.

Centenarian

Wilson, Jason. "How To Live Forever: Is the Secret to Be Found among the Centenarians in an Isolated Region of Sardinia?" *The Smart Set*. http://www.thesmartset.com/article/article08060709.aspx.

Buettner, Dan. *The Blue Zone: Lessons for Living Longer from the People Who've Lived the Longest*. Washington, DC: National Geographic, 2008.

Grierson, Bruce. What Makes Olga Run? *Parade*, December 29, 2013.

Woman's Health Initiative

Rillamas-Sun, Eileen, "Obesity and Late-Age Survival Without Major Disease or Disability in Older Women," *JAMA Internal Medicine* 174, no. 1 (2014): 98-106.

Recommended Reading

The Four Things That Matter Most by Ira Byock, MD
Published by Atria, June, 2014.

Western Attitudes toward Death: From the Middle Ages to the Present by Philippe Aries, translated by Patricia M. Ranum
Published by The Johns Hopkins University Press, 1974.

Acknowledgments

Thanks to Mary Abbott Waite, PhD, medical writer; Sheri Henry, MN, APRN-BC, palliative care coordinator, patient care coordinator at Piedmont Hospital in Atlanta, Georgia; Jerry Luxemburger, retired lawyer; and Florence B. Dawson, my partner and advisor; each for reading the manuscript and giving meaningful feedback.

About the Author

Jack Dawson, MD, is the director of cardiac rehabilitation at the Fuqua Heart Center of Piedmont Hospital in Atlanta, Georgia. He has been a practicing clinician in cardiology for more than forty years in Atlanta and has pioneered the use of social and psychological support in conjunction with physical rehabilitation in the secondary and primary prevention of chronic disease. He currently practices with Piedmont Heart Institute at Piedmont Hospital. He is a graduate of the Medical College of Georgia and completed his cardiology fellowship at Emory University School of Medicine Hospitals in Atlanta. *Choices*, his book self-published in 2013, is about stress as a risk factor for coronary artery disease and other illnesses. The book emphasizes that life and health depend on overcoming stressful issues for better health and relationships.

www.ingramcontent.com/pod-product-compliance
Lightning Source LLC
Chambersburg PA
CBHW070201100426
42743CB00013B/3008